ÍNDEX:

"THE WAY TO LIVE"

GEORGE HACKENSCHMIDT

George Hackenschmidt was a famous professional wrestler, weightlifter, writer, and sports philosopher, recognized as the first World Heavyweight Champion in wrestling history. Born in Dorpat, Russian Empire (now Tartu, Estonia), he was educated and began his sporting career in the city of Reval (now Tallinn) before training in St. Petersburg, Russia, under the tutelage of Wladislaw von Krajewski. However, he spent much of his life in London, where he became known by the nickname "The Russian Lion".

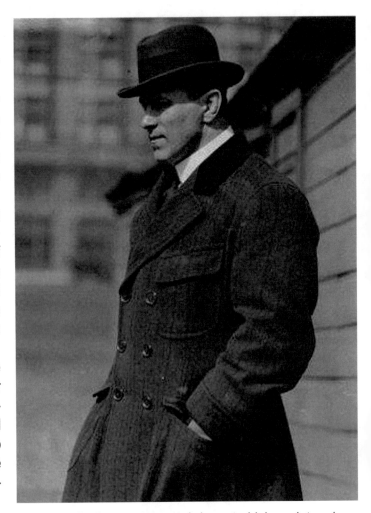

Hackenschmidt is credited with inventing the wrestling move known as the "Bear Hug" (a maneuver that became a cultural expression) and for being a pioneer of the "bench press" and the "hack squat" exercises. He was recognized for his impressive strength, physical condition, and flexibility. Later in his life, he wrote books on physical culture and training (such as the one you hold in your hands) and also delved into philosophy.

As a professional wrestler, Hackenschmidt gained fame by defeating the famous French wrestler Paul Pons for the European Championship (1898), winning the Russian Championship (1899), and claiming the World Championship in 1901 in Paris. He then traveled to England, where his career soared, and his name appeared in the marquees of major theaters and newspaper headlines.

His physical appearance, eloquence, culture, intellect, and success in the sport opened doors to high society, where he navigated naturally. Hackenschmidt later traveled to the United States, where, under Catch-As-Catch-Can rules, he defeated Tom Jenkins for the World Heavyweight Wrestling Championship at Madison Square Garden in 1905.

In 1908 and 1911, Hackenschmidt faced the American wrestling star Frank Gotch. These two legendary matches are among the most notable sporting events in early 20th-century American sports and helped propel wrestling's global popularity as entertainment. Hackenschmidt lost both matches to Gotch, and the circumstances of his defeat are still discussed today.

After returning to England, Hackenschmidt was preparing for a match against Stanislaus Zbyszko, but a knee injury that barely allowed him to walk became the perfect excuse for him to retire from professional wrestling and pursue other interests, such as philosophy, physical culture, and gardening.

Among his written works are: Complete Science of Wrestling (1909), Man and Cosmic Antagonism to Mind and Spirit (1935), Fitness and Your Self (1937), Consciousness and Character: True Definitions of Entity, Individuality, Personality, Nonentity (1937), The Way to Live in Health and Physical Fitness (1941), and The Three Memories and Forgetfulness: What They Are and What Their True Significance Is in Human.

In 1939, he became a French citizen after marrying Rachel Marie. In 1946, they moved to London, where they lived for the rest of their days. He remained in good physical shape into old age, and it is said that at 80, he still performed the bench press with 70 kilos and regularly ran 10 km. George Hackenschmidt passed away in 1968 at the age of 90.

WHY AM I MAKING THESE COMPILATIONS? JERONIMO MILO

I have always felt an irrational fascination with old photos, call it a fetish, an anchor to the past, or the need for everything to endure, I don't know, but every time I see an old black-and-white photo, I am moved to think about the story behind the people in it. What were they thinking? How did they manage to access that medium at that moment? Did they think that a simple photo would keep them alive until the present? All of these ideas are amplified when the photo shows something unique, ahead of its time, or transgressive for the historical moment. Sometimes the photo is a testament to a turning point in our history, and it can be something as incredible as the first time Chinese martial arts were exhibited in the West during a Nazi Olympics; or even a feat that has yet to be matched, like lifting an inhumanly heavy load, or a legendary fight that changed part of history.

Throughout my career, I've been asked (and criticized) a lot about why I write about the past. What's the need to write about a topic that's already buried, and for which, even today, more reliable information can be found through access to current books, studies, and trendy papers? I think that when we find someone ahead of their time (those characters who seem like they belong in the present and somehow took a time machine to the past), they can give us a good lesson on how to do things in the least favorable conditions. These writings are real "Monday journals" that warn us about things we haven't yet seen or that we've forgotten.

This book is like an immersion into the temporal abyss of wrestling and weightlifting. I also thought it was appropriate to include a list of personal reviews, explanations, translations, and a gallery of strongmen and strongwomen from the past to provide an adequate context of the era. *The Way of Life* is a work that goes beyond the world of training, diving deep into the most profound aspects of being human.

#lifehack

ATTENTION!!! THIS IS NOT A MODERN MANUAL!!!

This is neither a manual on Powerlifting, bodybuilding, Olympic lifting, nor mixed martial arts. It is a work of historical analysis and compilation! So, if you're expecting a modern book with color photos and computer-generated graphics, it's time to put it down right now.

This compilation is based on the original manual by George Hackenschmidt from 1908/1911 (1941?), and I have removed nothing to remain faithful to the original work. Many terms and concepts you'll encounter may be shocking to today's social consensus. There is virtually no mention of women's training, and you might find terminology that is now outdated but was normalized at the time, without this reflecting any real negative stance by the author toward any social group or individual.

The book is filled with my personal annotations, where I will not only translate the ideas but also the language and the means by which the foundations of modern strength training, as we know it today, were developed. Many of the exercises in this manual come directly from the original book. So, you should only practice them under the supervision of a professional and with the authorization of a doctor.

FOREWORD

By an unknown author (from the 1941 edition).

George Hackenschmidt, the author of this book was one of the greatest Strength athletes the world has ever seen. Best known as the world's champion wrestler in the early years of this century, he was also famous as a strong man and all around athlete.

His first specialty was cycling, in which he won numerous prizes. Wrestling and weight lifting were the chief sports during the indoor season, which was quite lengthy in Russia, where he then lived.

While still in his teens, he excelled in world records, and later throughout his career, created records in strength feats and lifting which either stand today or have been beaten by the smallest of margins. He excelled at swimming, jumping, and running— in short, at any line of physical endeavor. When he visited this country, late in his wrestling career, he illustrated his agility by jumping over a series of six rubbing tables and turning a forward somersault with a pair of 50-pound dumbbells in his hands. Most unusual and difficult feats.

He is considered to be the greatest wrestler of modern times at real wrestling. Butting, foot twisting, and tricks which are now a part of wrestling came into popularity or use about the time Hackenschmidt retired from the game of wrestling.

Hackenschmidt lived a most unusual and colorful life. He traveled the world, knew intimately presidents and kings. Well-educated, in later years he became a writer and lecturer on philosophy. His recent photo shows him as he appeared on a visit to this country in the summer of 1939. He was here to lecture on philosophy at Harvard and Yale universities.

He's an outstanding example of the old Greek adage, "A sound mind in a sound body", or its modern counterpart, the Strength and Health magazine slogan, Devoted to the Culture of Mind and Body. His great success at strength sports, lifting, wrestling, and other athletics, his splendid condition at present with a minimum of physical training during these last 35 years, best illustrates that he "knows whereof he speaks," and really knows "the way to live."

When you follow the advice of George Hackenschmidt, you take instruction from a man who has done things, a man who follows his own system of living with great success, as you too can do. His is not a case of "do as I say," but "do as I do and have done." Born a Russian, Hackenschmidt married a French woman and is now a citizen of France.

This book is considered to be the largest-selling Physical Training Book of all time. It is in its 21st large printing. The best proof of its excellence and the splendid results many thousands of men and women have received from the instruction it contains. It should be in the library of every strength and health-seeking man or woman.

HOW TO READ THIS MANUAL (AND THE 1900S ERA)

Here are some specific translations, terminology, measurements, and elements of the time and place that will help us better understand this text and its context.

MEASUREMENTS
1 Pound = 0.453 kilograms.
1 Stone = 14 pounds = 6.350 kilograms.
1 Inch = 2.54 centimeters.

ABBREVIATIONS
N. de J.M. = Note by Jerónimo Milo.
N. del T. = Translator's note.

The "half Nelson"

Perhaps the most used and favorite wrestling technique of Hack in this manual. In this move, one hand passes under the opponent's armpit while holding their head. The other hand can either hold another part of the opponent's body or reinforce the half Nelson grip.

OLD IMPLEMENTS

Here we have some implements, many of which are still used today in their original form or modified, while others have simply fallen into disuse. The globes or spheres, so typical of this era, could be solid as part of the bar or hollow, allowing them to be filled with sand, pellets, clay, or water.

DUMBBELL

SOLID DUMBBEL

HOLLOW DUMBBELL TO FILL WITH DISCS, SAND, CLAY, OR WATER

HOW TO READ THE REVIEWS OF THE "MASTERS OF STRENGTH"?

In this work, I extend the profiles of the ancient strongmen and strongwomen in sections we will refer to as MASTERS OF STRENGTH (MDS).

KNOWN NAME + (Birth name).

ALIAS: Modified or artistic name.

ORIGIN: City and country.

PERIOD: ANCESTRAL (UNTIL 1799), ANCIENT (1800-1860), CLASSIC (1860-1914), MODERN (1914-1970), CURRENT (1979 - PRESENT).

SPECIALTY: Their main focus.

SPECIAL SKILL: The skill that made them famous and in which they excelled.

FAMOUS QUOTE: A phrase or thought that defines their persona.

HIGHLIGHT: The most important event or achievement of their life.

ANTAGONIST: Enemy. Rival or opponent.

PREFERRED ELEMENT: Favorite training, competition, or exhibition tool.

LEGACY: Students or followers they left behind. Influence and impact on the history of physical culture.

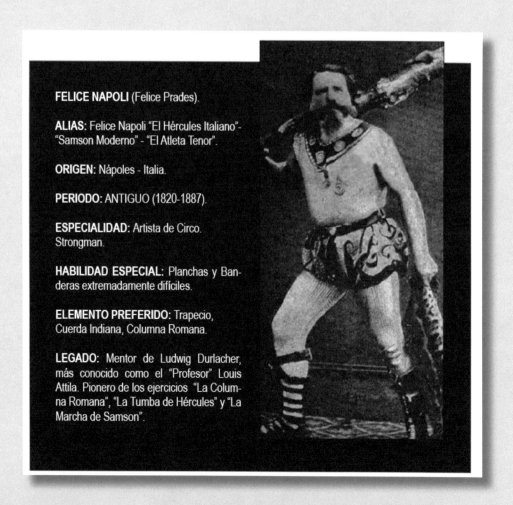

FELICE NAPOLI (Felice Prades).

ALIAS: Felice Napoli "El Hércules Italiano" - "Samson Moderno" - "El Atleta Tenor".

ORIGEN: Nápoles - Italia.

PERIODO: ANTIGUO (1820-1887).

ESPECIALIDAD: Artista de Circo. Strongman.

HABILIDAD ESPECIAL: Planchas y Banderas extremadamente difíciles.

ELEMENTO PREFERIDO: Trapecio, Cuerda Indiana, Columna Romana.

LEGADO: Mentor de Ludwig Durlacher, más conocido como el "Profesor" Louis Attila. Pionero de los ejercicios "La Columna Romana", "La Tumba de Hércules" y "La Marcha de Samson".

CHAPTER I

The way of living in health and physical condition.
Introduction.

This not at all improbable that many persons will raise objections to the title of this book, on the ground that the Road of Life which I may point out is by no means one which the average person would wish to tread. These will very probably suggest (without having troubled to read these pages) that they have no desire to distinguish themselves either as wrestlers or as weight-lifters, and that in consequence Hackenschmidt's Way of Life must necessarily diverge pretty considerably from theirs.

But, as will be seen, it has not been my design to confine myself to laying down a series of rules for strong men and athletes only: my object in writing this book has been rather to lay before my readers such data as may enable them to secure Health as well as Strength.

It is true that a large section is devoted to exercises, etc., which will tend to the development of Strength, but then, surely, it is the desire of every man to increase his physical powers. Health can never be divorced from Strength. The second is an inevitable sequel to the first. A man can only fortify himself against disease by strengthening his body in such manner as will enable it to defy the attacks of any malady.

The progress of civilisation has been chiefly marked by the progress of Medical Science. The study and practice of Surgery and Medicine have grown amazingly during the past few generations. Sanitary arrangements have been almost perfected, while the precautions and safeguards against disease, which have been instituted by states and municipalities, are simply admirable.

Despite all these improvements, one can scarcely come across any official health report which does not bewail an all-round degeneration of physique.

There are fewer plagues and pestilences, but there would appear to be an infinitely greater number of sickly, weedy, stunted people than there used to be.

The reason is not far to seek. There is a universal urban immigration, a vast increase in the numbers of those who are engaged in indoor and sedentary occupation, and only here and there is any attempt made to combat the consequent unhealthy conditions of life with the only satisfactory weapon, Rational Physical Exercise.

Unfortunately, the majority of people seem to associate the words Physical Culture with huge muscular development. Men who do not entertain any ambition of figuring as professional athletes consequently omit to pay any attention to the care of their bodies.

They do not wish to be ill, but they nevertheless appear to consider that occasional ill-health is the inevitable fate of every son of Adam and must be endured, if not exactly welcomed.

Now, apart from extraordinary causes, there is absolutely no reason why any man should ever be ill, as long as he keeps his body so physically fit as to safeguard it against any breakdown. Fifteen or twenty minutes' daily exercise will be all-sufficient for this purpose. Surely no very heavy price to pay for such a valuable result.

This is no idle, unfounded claim, Any reader who may fancy it to be such, need but make, say, a fortnight's experiment of the course prescribed. Even before that period expired, the beneficial result would be readily perceived.

The exercise, however, must be rational, suitable exercise. Movements such as will tune up the whole frame and keep every organ and muscle working harmoniously together.

I do not claim to be the first preacher of this gospel, nor could I venture to pose as such, seeing the vast library of books which have been published from time to time, on this subject of Physical Culture and its advantages. But from a more or less complete study of the said works I have come to the conclusion that the vast majority of them, or at all events of the most instructive ones, have been so written as to be largely unintelligible to "the man in the street," while others, and these, unfortunately, by no means the least popular, deal almost exclusively with systems of exercise which their authors have never practised themselves, nor which, to my knowledge, have ever been practised by any really strong man.

I have, therefore, confined myself to dealing only with such systems of exercise, diet, rest, etc., as my own observation and experience have shown thoroughly sound and reliable, proved to be such in numberless instances, and in describing them have sought to set down my views in such language as will be readily comprehended by every reader, avoiding as far as possible all unnecessary technical details. Whether I have failed or succeeded in these endeavours remains for my readers to judge.

ANOTHER AHEAD OF HIS TIME?

Beyond the nuances that the works of the ancient Strongmen may have, anyone who reads these works agrees on one point: they were ahead of their time. Only someone who takes these books, methods, and thoughts out of context will mock them as archaic or outdated. For example, an old photograph of a barbell squat from the early 1900s may seem of low quality to the modern reader. However, one must not forget that modern squats probably wouldn't exist if these pioneers hadn't developed those "ancient" squats. Thanks to that beginning, significant progress has been made in both equipment and knowledge in recent years.

Of all these early authors, Hackenschmidt is perhaps a special case. In his texts, we see a communion between strength, train-ing, wrestling, and very importantly (since it gives the title to this work) the way of life. As his career progressed, he went through all possible stages: he was a strongman, a wrestler, a preacher of healthy living, and even delved into the highest aspects of man, from the moral to the philosophical. Hackenschmidt was fascinated by function-al strength that could be applied to wres-tling and to improving daily life. This set him apart from the bodybuilders of the time and from the showmen who performed simply to entertain the public. His approach allowed him to view strength training as a holistic tool, one that could be used as a true way of life. After establishing the foundations of strength training, he turned to more meta-physical and existential aspects, proving his interest in the evolutionary development of the human being.

There is one point on which I would wish to lay stress, and that is, that no matter what age a man may have attained, he is by no means too old to commence exercise. I have devoted several pages to exercises with heavy weights, for the purpose of developing Strength (with a capital S), and I sincerely hope that none of my readers will be frightened on this account. It may be suggested that there is no reason why a man should go to the trouble and exertion of struggling with heavy weights, since there is no crying necessity for that particular man to acquire any phenomenal degree of strength.

To that I would reply by asking why a man should desire to be weak? He was endowed by his Creator with muscles and sinews which would enable him to cope successfully with such physical feats as he might be faced with during his earthly career.

Modern social conditions have deprived him of that open-air life and hard physical exertion which would have kept these muscles and sinews in good condition and sound working order.

But since he has been separated from the natural physical advantages, which were freely offered to him in bygone centuries, he should surely avail himself of the efficient substitutes which are offered to him by trained and practised physical culturists and the method of which I have here endeavoured to set forth.

For it is only by exercising with heavy weights that any man can hope to develop really great strength. He should of course combine these exercises with skipping, running, jumping and gymnastics of every description in order to similarly develop his activity and agility, but, unless he sedulously carries out the bar-bell and dumb-bell exercises as well, he can never acquire really great Physical powers.

The man of forty or fifty, however, who has passed the age when the desire for great strength is still active and who only desires the acquisition and preservation of health may content himself with the exercises designed solely for that end.

But I would strongly urge on all such, that it is their bounden duty to encourage, by every means in their power, the pursuit of Strength among all the youths of their district. Persuade the boys and young men in every locality to band themselves together for the purpose of forming Physical Culture Clubs and Gymnasia, where they can exercise and develop their bodies.

Enthusiasm will soon be evoked. The public-houses and other even less desirable resorts will suffer (no bad result this); the country and the human race will benefit; nor will the minds of the youths in question lack a sympathetic development.

The old notion that physical prowess was inseparable from a dull intelligence is completely exploded, and happily so, seeing that it was about the most harmful notion which has ever been entertained by man.

A boy whose attention is directed to physical exercise will speedily recognize its benefits and healthful pleasures, and will consequently readily and instinctively avoid all harmful excesses. He will also inevitably develop an interest in his own anatomy and thereby in what are now known as "the mysteries of life"; soon, it is to be hoped (by the spread of Physical Culture), to become less mysterious than they have been hitherto.

THE "INVENTOR" OF THE BENCH PRESS?

To qualify someone as the "inventor" of an exercise is an oversimplification. It is very difficult to pinpoint the person or people responsible for such an iconic exercise as the bench press. Nonetheless, Hackenschmidt was one of the first to describe this technique and all its variations in his version of the floor press (horizontal press from the floor). He was recognized in his time for holding records with this technique before the migration of this exercise to the bench itself. In the photo, we see one of the versions with a bridge over the head, with a direct transfer to the capabilities of freestyle wrestling.

CHAPTER II
Why should we be strong?

Is a well-known fact that the majority of men today are relatively weak, whereas the struggle for existence demands now more than at any previous epoch that we should all be strong!

The reader may think that physical strength is not a necessity, but I will try and prove to him that man cannot derive real enjoyment from life unless he possesses a powerful and healthy physical constitution. A famous physician expressed himself as follows: "If I think of my experiences during a thirty years' practice, I cannot recall many cases where a patient became ill through too great an exertion on his physical system, whereas I remember many hundreds who have contracted serious illness through mental strain and brain fag, and their complete recovery invariably was a slow and difficult process.

"I have come to the distinct conclusion, that the physical constitution of the human frame never was intended merely for study, but rather for manual and bodily exercise. I have found that those who have lived an active outdoor life have retained and enjoyed a brightness born of health far longer than others. Such people always enjoyed their meals, seldom suffered from indigestion, headaches, or nervous exhaustion. Indigestion is the direct result of the ineffective performance by the digestive organs of their functions, brought on either, on the one hand, by over-eating or consuming unsuitable food and noxious drugs, or, on the other hand, by physical inactivity. What a contrast to these are the constitutions of those people who toil in rooms or do mental work only; they often suffer from heat in the head, cold feet, sluggish digestion, or weak and inactive bowels. Few among them are those who do not suffer from some form of nervous complaint. The feeling of comfort and happiness is almost unknown to them.

"We know that every organ, when actively performing its duties, demands a rich supply of blood; its veins become enlarged, and, considering the fact that much more blood flows through a muscle while it is in activity than while it is at rest, it is evident that the same rule holds good as regards the brain. If more blood flows to the brain than under normal conditions, the other parts of the body are more or less depleted of it, feet and arms become cold, and the feeling is, to say the least, uncomfortable. I have the firm conviction that in time every one will recognize the necessity of daily bodily exercises in one form or another, as an ordinary counterpart to one's daily mental exertions."

Human life is not unlike a commercial business establishment. There is a continual exchange of matter, and just as the commercial establishment suffers and decays when the turnover diminishes, or the stock of goods accumulates without being disposed of, so a continuous exchange of matter is needful for our body, if a paralysis in life's activity—in another word, illness—is to be averted or a complete stoppage—that is death—prevented. Just as a commercial business flourishes the more this interchange of goods takes place, so a man benefits in health and comfort and can get out of himself better service in any useful direction, if the exchange of matter in his body takes place regularly and frequently. In life, however, cause and effect continually change their role. As the man of commerce must not be idle, but must be active from early morn till night, so we can only keep our wonderful organism in constant regularity by repeated impulse to, and continual exertion in, its respective functions. This is the only way to prevent exhaustion of the organs and to contribute properly to their strengthening, improvement, and preservation. You will ask how far we can attain this, and how it is possible to effect such a deep influence on a whole life's activity. I would reply to this in the following manner:

Every movement is produced by the muscles. These are skeins of flesh tissues, which have the vital faculty of contraction and extension. They are attached by sinews to the foundation of bone, and by contraction they change in position or alter in shape. The impulse to this movement is carried by the nerves, which have their centre in the brain. The nerves are not unlike the metal

20

"Health can never be divorced from strength."

wires of a battery, which carry the electricity whither it is needed, and in like manner the brain sends the impulse by means of the nerves to whatever muscles it wills. If, therefore, the muscles are frequently set in motion by our will, they are first of all strengthened in their power of contraction and of executing different movements and are thus brought to their full development and perfection.

FELICE NAPOLI (Felice Prades)

Alias: Felice Napoli "The Italian Hercules" - "Modern Samson" - "The Tenor Athlete"

Origin: Naples, Italy

Period: Ancient (1820–1887)

Specialty: Circus Performer Strongman

Special skill: Extremely difficult planks and flags

Preferred elements: Trapeze, Indian Rope, Roman Column

Legacy: Mentor of Ludwig Durlacher, better known as "Professor" Louis Attila. Pioneer of exercises such as "The Roman Column," "Hercules' Tomb," and "Samson's March".

Those muscles which are left inactive to a greater or lesser extent lose their power of contraction and naturally deteriorate. This retrogression appears in the shape of muscular weakness and exhaustion. We find these effects mostly among people of the so-called upper classes. They are tired by the least exertion, are afraid of the slightest draught, and are often martyrs to weak nerves, rheumatism, and catarrh. Ladies who take no regular physical exercise,

Felice Napoli was a 19th-century Italian strongman who played a crucial role in the history of Physical Culture.

He is considered by many historians as "The First Strongman" and is perhaps even more famous for being the mentor of "Professor" Louis Attila, who in turn mentored Eugen Sandow. Thus, if Sandow is regarded as the "Father of Bodybuilding," one could argue that Felice Napoli is the "Great-Grandfather of Physical Culture." Undoubtedly, Napoli is one of those "Unsung Heroes" who deserves to be studied and remembered.

Born in 1821 under the surname Prades in Naples, Italy, Felice Napoli built his career as a circus performer in Paris, eventually reaching the most prestigious circuses and music halls across Europe. He began as a weightlifter and specialized in kettlebell juggling. As his strength increased, he added numerous spectacular feats to his repertoire, including "Hercules' Tomb" (holding a 50-centimeter-thick rock on his chest in a supine quadrupedal position while en-

during the blow of a sledgehammer to break it), "Samson's March" (walking with weights strapped to his neck, belt, ankles, and carrying a barbell on his shoulders—a precursor to modern weighted carries), as well as performing extremely difficult planks and flags on the "Roman column", "Indian rope", and trapeze.

Napoli was a master of the stage. According to French historian Edmund Desbonnet, Felice was "particularly notable for his artistic talent and the way he presented his act". A true showman, Napoli also had a beautiful singing voice and performed under the pseudonym "The Tenor Athlete". At the time, strength feats were often presented as part of small scenes or pantomimes, with lifts integrated into the storyline.

His peak fame came during his performances with the Wallshlager Circus in the 1850s. He retired in 1877 and lived for a time in Berlin.

Felice Napoli passed away ten years later in London, on July 28, 1887, at the age of 66.

or who are not engaged in any occupation entailing such, are invariably startled and frightened by the least unexpected noise, such as the sudden opening of a door. They become "nervous" and often hysterically affected by unlooked-for occurrences of even the most paltry nature. Now all these ills and disorders are unknown to those who take regular physical exercise, for by it their nervous system obtains strength and firmness and that endurance which is the essence of a good constitution.

LOUIS ATTILA (Ludwig Durlacher).

Alias: "Professor" Louis Attila - "The lion athlete"

Origin: Karlsruhe, Germany

Period: Ancient (1844–1924)

Specialty: Weightlifter - strongman - trainer

Notable skill: Trainer of champions

Famous quote: "I will donate 1000 dollars to any charitable foundation of your choice if i cannot conclusively prove that every individual claiming to be a physical culture instructor in this country (united states) has either been my pupil or studied one of the systems I originated, perfected, and published." [1894]

Preferred equipment: dumbbells, barbells, roman bench

Highlight: performed his strongman show during queen victoria's golden jubilee in 1887. founded the first physical culture gym in the united states in 1898, "Attila's athletic studio & school of physical culture"

LEGACY OF ATTILA:

- Made invaluable contributions to the Physical Culture movement in Europe and the United States during the late 19th and early 20th centuries.

- A pioneer in the use of weight training to enhance performance in professional athletes.

- Innovator of "Personalized Training" for the wealthy and famous.

- Advocated for equal opportunities for women in sports, particularly in weightlifting and boxing.

- Publicly stated that weight training slows the aging process nearly 100 years before the medical community reached the same conclusion.

- Mentor and trainer of Eugene Sandow.

- Creator of the "Bent Press," then known as "screwing."

- First to introduce the barbell with interchangeable weight plates, a tool universally used today.

- Developed the "2.5 kg Dumbbell Exercises" system, published in 1913 and designed for beginners.

Louis Attila, known as "The Professor," was one of the most significant figures in Physical Culture. According to most authorities in the field, he is considered the TRUE "Father of Bodybuilding", as he was the mentor and trainer of Eugene Sandow. Sandow later became a public icon and undoubtedly the greatest "ambassador" of bodybuilding.

Attila received an excellent formal education in Berlin, where he not only developed his intellect but also learned to play the piano and became fluent in five languages. From a young age, he showed an interest in physical prowess, leading him to study acrobatics and gymnastics. The most significant moment of his childhood was meeting the famous Italian strongman Felice Napoli, who accepted him as a pupil. Under Napoli's mentorship, he mastered the craft,

Through the pressure of blood and the accumulation of nerve fluid in the brain, the nervous man is filled with continual anxiety for his physical well-being. His overstrung nerves cause him to imagine all kinds of ailments. One thought after another flits across his mind; at one time he believes himself to be strong, at another weak, now he fancies himself well, now ill. He is tormented by a never-ending strife between hope of life and fear of death. Hope after hope slips successively from his grasp, and finally he sinks into a more or less dangerous mental illness, the result of which may easily lead him to seek release in self-destruction.

learning both feats of strength and the art of stage presentation. At 17, he continued his training at the Baden Shooting Sports Club, excelling in swimming and athletics.

At 19, in 1863, Attila began his career as a strongman, touring Europe with various circuses, sometimes performing solo and other times paired with a renowned strongwoman known as "Valerie, The Gladiator." His professional success on stage and outstanding sports performances attracted many prominent members of European high society. This led to his role as the "personal trainer" of the rich and famous. Among his students were key figures of European royalty and nobility, as well as notable millionaires of the era. His clients included Tsar Alexander III of Russia, King Edward VII of England, Baron Edmond de Rothschild, and Cornelius Vanderbilt.

In 1886, Attila opened his first public gym in Brussels, Belgium. It was there that a young Friedrich Mueller (later known as Eugene Sandow) began his training.

In 1887, Attila reached the peak of his showman career by performing at the Golden Jubilee celebration of Queen Victoria of England.

In 1893, Attila emigrated to the United States at the invitation of famed publisher Richard K. Fox with the goal of opening a new gym in New York. In 1898, he founded the legendary "Attila's Athletic Studio & School of Physical Culture," where he established weightlifting as a method to enhance the performance of professional athletes. He also became a major advocate for equal opportunities for women in sports, particularly in weightlifting and boxing.

Just as he had in Europe, Attila continued to work as a personal trainer for prominent figures in the United States, including Supreme Court members, famous artists,

The most effectual means of preventing all the disadvantages and evil consequences of a neglected exercise of body and muscles is methodical physical training.

Just as the man of sedentary habits and weak body possesses a correspondingly sluggish mind and lack of energy, so he who assiduously pursues a physical development gains not only that desired government of his organs, but in marked degree obtains a thorough mastery of his will and, consequently, an easy and contented mind.

The frequent employment of one's will power masters all organs of movement and trains them to perform feats which otherwise would have been difficult, painful, and even impossible. The man becomes independent and self-reliant; he will never be a coward, and, when real danger threatens, he is the one who is looked up to by others. The knowledge of one's strength entails a real mastery over oneself; it breeds energy and courage, helps one over the most difficult tasks of life, and procures contentment and true enjoyment of living. Who would still lag behind in inactivity and weakness?

and powerful bankers. His mentorship extended to numerous renowned strongmen and athletes. Along with Eugene Sandow, notable protégés included Lionel Strongfort, Louis Cyr, Horace Barre, Warren Lincoln Travis, and others.

In 1913, Attila published his "2.5 kg Dumbbell Exercises" system, which he had developed during his time at the Baden Shooting Sports Club. Originally designed as an introductory course for beginners, its popularity transformed it into the foundation for daily training in the armies of several European countries.

As if that were not enough, Attila was the creator of the "Bent Press," the inventor of the "Roman Bench," and the first to introduce the concept of using barbells with adjustable weight plates.

Attila continued lifting weights until the age of 77, remaining a great strongman until his death on March 15, 1925.

CHAPTER III

Adaptability and characteristics

I SHOULD like to say a few words upon this subject, and I know that I echo the opinions of well-known authorities on training.

It is natural that a sound constitution, inherited from healthy parents, and a proportionate build, should be great advantages for a future athlete. Especially should the heart and the lungs be normal, although I quite admit that one finds strong and healthy children of comparatively weak parents, and vice versa; and I know of many cases in which seemingly weak or ailing youngsters have developed into strong men, thanks to their energetic endurance and steadfast desire to achieve that result.

As regards stature, I will only mention that a moderate height of from 5ft. 6in. to 6ft. seems very favourable, seeing that that is the average of most strong men (I myself am 5ft. 9¾in.); but, of course, there are exceptions to this. The body should be built very uniformly, so that the whole appearance makes a harmonious impression. It would not matter much whether the arms or legs were somewhat under the normal length, but a short trunk would indicate a poor development of the important inner organs, such as lungs, heart, and stomach, and, therefore, would be less favourable. For wrestling and boxing, long arms are an advantage, whilst for weight-lifting I should prefer shorter arms, but, of course, the principal point lies with the more or less favourable leverage capacity of the frame.

Now it is a fact that by reasonable physical exercise the growth of the structure is encouraged; by reasonable exercise I mean such as is adapted to the personal constitution and the age of the individual.

During the process of growth and bodily development, say until about the twentieth year, one ought not to practise any extreme athletic feats, but ought to pay chief attention to agility and alertness. Regular exercise in youth stimulates the growth and increases the strength and efficiency of all internal processes.

For great feats of strength with heavy weights experience teaches that between the years of thirty and forty is the most favourable age; I suppose though, that I am an exception, as I had already established world's records before I was twenty-one. It will, however, I think, be of interest to quote the opinions of a few eminent authorities on these subjects.

ADOLPH ANDRUSCHKEWITZSCH, who is a well-known Russian athlete and authority on Physical Culture, of Reval, says: "Every country can produce strong men; Estland (Russia) in general offers no special advantages, although one might argue that Estland, similarly to, perhaps, Eastern Prussia (the native country of Sandow, Sturm, and Siegfried), has few industries, and that therefore its inhabitants pursue their vocations principally in the open, breathe pure air, and live on healthy, unadulterated foods. Estland's percentage of people of consumptive tendencies is very low, just as is that of Eastern Prussia; while in the thickly-populated kingdom of Saxony the ravages of this terrible disease are very severe. At the same time, however, Arthur Saxon, who is undoubtedly the best weight-lifter of the present time, hails from Saxony! (This opinion expressed in 1910)

"To become a good athlete the candidate should, in my opinion, be possessed of a strong-boned frame and a good sound chest, and he should be generally healthy. To attain this, he ought to avoid worry and strenuous daily toil; the choice of food is of secondary consideration, as long as his meals are wholesome, regular, and properly digested. Alcohols and stimulants may produce seeming momentary strength, but in reality they weaken the system. An essential point is, that the candidate puts his life and soul into the study of proper training; enduring will power is the mightiest factor for good results, and for the production of men like Hackenschmidt, Lurich, Sandow, Saxon, Aberg, or Hoeppener."

MAX DANTHAGE, of Vienna, the well-known athlete-gymnast, says: "My principal nourishment consists of meat. I drink very little. For my breakfast I take very weak tea and a buttered roll. With my luncheon and dinner about one pint of light beer; I never drink wines, spirits or water. Except in summer, I do not bathe often, but I wash and take douches frequently, and use the towel well. I never fail to go through this washing performance after every exertion which has produced perspiration, and I may add that I use cold water. This cold washing should, however, not be of longer duration than a few seconds, if the body has been perspiring. As regards training, I recommend the following items:

APOLLON

Marsillargues, France [1862-1928]

Louis Uni, famously known as "The Mighty Apollon", was a French strongman renowned for his exceptional grip strength. Coming from a family of tall individuals, he had an imposing physique, standing at 1.90 meters tall—significantly above the average French height of 1.63 meters in the 1800s. Apollon was mentored by Edmond Desbonnet, a champion and scholar in Physical Education, who recognized his natural talent. He enjoyed a successful career as a strongman, performing theatrical feats of strength, such as "escaping" from a cell by bending its bars and lifting exceptionally heavy or oversized weights with ease and grace.

Much of his success was attributed to his natural physique, as it was said that he never adhered to a strict training program.

One of the highlights of his act was the use of a unique weight known as "The Apollon Wheel," a specially crafted barbell with train wagon wheels as its ends. It featured a 5 cm diameter axle and weighed 166 kg. Publicized as "unliftable", it became a hallmark of his performances.

Apollon's legacy in the world of strongmen is more closely tied to the concept of "innate strength" rather than the product of systematic training, making him a legendary figure of natural power.

"Moderation in everything, of whatever nature.

Daily short baths and vigorous rubbing down.

Daily physical exercise, avoiding great feats of strength but performing feats of endurance, and this until one begins to perspire slightly.

I began to practise physical exercises regularly and systematically six years ago, when I was thirty-one. Of course, I went through the usual physical training at school, between the years of six and seventeen, and after this I continued gymnastics a few times per week on the horizontal bar at home in the garden and practised with small dumb-bells. I like swimming, and have always indulged

VULCANA

Abergavenny, Wales [1874-1946].

Miriam Kate Williams, known as Vulcana, was a Welsh strongwoman who toured the United Kingdom, Europe, and Australia, performing in theaters and exhibitions where she showcased her feats of strength.
While some of her demonstrations were exaggerated or involved tricks, Vulcana also achieved many legitimate feats and lifts that had never been performed by a woman before, such as the bent press and "The Tomb of Hercules".
She became an icon of female strength and an advocate for gender equality. In addition to demonstrating her bent press by using men as weights, she was a vocal opponent of corsets and any clothing that negatively impacted women's bodies.

in this pleasurable exercise when I had an opportunity. Skating and cycling were other hobbies, and anything appertaining to gymnastical sports, except fencing and riding. I have never made a study of any particular line of sport. My present endeavour is to develop my body in every direction, and so give it every day not only its necessary food, but also to exercise it until, as I said before, my pores open and perspiration commences. The precise observation of all these points fitted me for such feats of endurance as you are familiar with, and my hardihood has become proverbial among my friends and acquaintances. I have been called the man who never catches cold or catarrh, and who is never ill. My measurements are: Height, 5ft. 8in.; chest, deflated, 36½in., normal, 37½in., inflated, 40¾in.; thighs, 24¾in.; calves, 15in.; biceps, 14¾in.; wrist, 7½in.; weight, 159lb."

I must draw the reader's attention to the fact that Danthage, who is a member of the Royal Opera Band, is the gymnast who, among other feats of endurance, made what the Germans call the deep knee-bend 6,000 times during four consecutive hours. The "knee-bend" is a capital exercise, and consists in bending your knees outwards by moving from the erect position to a sort of sitting posture without moving the feet.

MONSIEUR GASTNER, the well-known athlete of Barnum and Bailey's Circus, writes: "Lots of people ask me whether they can become strong. Most certainly! You all can acquire great strength, if you have the will and proper guidance. But before all you must cultivate will power, and this first lesson is the most important one. If physical exercises alone, without your will and mind, were all that was needful, every one could become a strong man, whether he be a brain or muscle worker.

"The labourer, however, who never particularly uses his mind while he strains all his muscles in hard toil, and every day lifts weights, does not necessarily augment his strength.

"Those who would like to have well-developed muscles should guard against over-exertion and impetuous exercise. One can become strong by daily exercises with heavy dumb-bells, and such exercises should take place either two hours before or after meals. Before one begins with heavier weights, one ought to

HERMANN GOERNER

Saxony, Germany [1891-1956].

Hermann Goerner was a German strong-man who toured Europe, the United Kingdom, and South Africa with Pagel's Circus. He achieved feats of strength that remain unmatched to this day, particularly in lifts requiring exceptional grip strength.

Goerner began lifting weights at the age of 10. By 14, he could perform a one-handed swing with 50 kg. His impressive physique also made him a sought-after model for painters and sculptors.

After World War I, despite losing an eye in combat, Goerner continued lifting weights and became a professional strongman. In his circus act, he would "wrestle" a young elephant, perform a 105 kg cross-armed snatch, and challenge members of the audience to lift a 150 kg dumbbell with a 6 cm diameter handle— a classic "challenge dumbbell" typical of the strongman world.

Some of his most notable feats of strength include a 177 kg clean and press, a 77 kg one-arm snatch, a 200 kg two-hands any-how lift, and his favorite lift, the deadlift.

Although today's world record exceeds 500 kg, it is worth noting that Goerner managed a 360 kg deadlift in an era without ergogenic aids. He also earned a Guinness World Record by performing a one-handed dead-lift with 306 kg.

Goerner injured his hand in an accident in 1929, which affected his training, but he continued to lift until the onset of World War II. Toward the end of the war, he was captured and sent to a Soviet concentration camp. Later, he returned to Germany and retired with his wife in a small village near Hannover. Hermann "The Mighty" Goerner passed away in 1956 at the age of 65.

study what weights would not cause over exertion for the constitution as it then is. I recommend cold baths twice a week, or daily cold washing of the whole body with a sponge, and this immediately upon rising in the morning. This is very healthy and invigorating.

"I should advise an amateur to vary the duration of his exercises; for instance, if he feels particularly fit he may exercise a little longer than on days when he feels more or less tired.

"There is no doubt that simple food is the best."

CHAPTER IV
Physical perfection and strength

NOW propose to lay before you my own views as to the most direct method of gaining physical perfection, strength and dexterity. There are a good many works in existence on training and physical culture, especially in England. Among these there are some very useful ones, but I have missed in most of them certain rules which are indispensable for the attainment of a high degree of strength. I do not propose to weary you with strange expressions and scientific language, but I wish to make you acquainted with a system to which I owe my own strength, and under which ALL other well-known strong men have trained. In the first instance, I would have you observe the following very important rules, the neglect of which in any system, even my own, would decrease its value:—

DO YOU WISH TO BECOME STRONG?

Certainly, you will answer, that is my intention, that is my wish; to which I should reply that a simple wishing will not do it. You must want to—in other words, you must act. You have no idea how much stress I lay on this first condition! The will I should call that incessant inward impulse which spurs one on to the goal. The beginning is difficult, and many a man gets no further than the initial stages. He is not unlike the would-be piano virtuoso, who, after a few lessons, comes to the point when the exercises become more difficult and tedious, when he throws them up altogether. Others, again, put exercises off from day to day by taking firm mental resolutions to begin in earnest and to make up for lost time, on the morrow—which seldom comes.

The question whether anyone can become strong I answer emphatically in the affirmative. I could mention dozens of cases where men of an already advanced age (40 to 60), and under the most difficult circumstances, have acquired quite a considerable increase of strength by physical culture. I have already pointed out that increase of strength means betterment of health and increase of comfort, so that every man must profit by such increase of strength, even if he does not intend to acquire it for professional or other pecuniary purposes.

Believe me, excuses which a man may advance such as, "I am too old," "I have not sufficient time," "My position or my business does not permit," etc., are all mere subterfuges to cover a weak will power. The Britons have a splendid proverb, "Where there's a will there's a way," and I am a staunch believer in it.

Now, I quite admit that to produce an extraordinarily strong man (or woman) very many favourable conditions are necessary, but I sincerely trust that the coming generation will average a physical perfection such as that now displayed by athletes. If so this will be due to the rational physical culture and care of the body, which deservedly finds every day fresh adherents. The determination to become strong is indispensable for success, and the best proof of this is that among the masses of hard toilers, however strange it may seem, we do not find very strong people, certainly not in the measure one might expect. As a wrestler I have had an opportunity of discovering strong men in all positions of life. Manual labour alone is therefore not the source of strength. All prominent strong men have fostered their strength by the aid of a strong will power; they wanted to become strong, and consequently succeeded.

I remember a photographer in Germany who confessed to me that although in his youth he was a great enthusiast for physical culture, yet, when he realized that he would have to be a conscript, the idea of which was not only distasteful but even dreadful to him, he neglected the exercises he had once pursued, with the absolute intention of becoming unfit and exempt from service—in which he succeeded. Here is a case of a man who wished not to be strong, and who exerted his will power to that end. The result he attained was, that from his appearance I should call him a withered individual. If a man can to such an extent exercise his will against nature, how much more can he do so to foster a natural process?

As further evidence of the influence of the 'Will to Develop Weakness," may be instanced the case of the Russian Jews, among whom military service is most unpopular. In fact the vast majority of Russian Jews seek to evade their military service by every means in their power, and find that the only really efficacious method is by being physically unfit. Now, as is well known, the Jews as a people are one of the healthiest in the world, and one, moreover, which has turned out a very large number of prominent athletes. The Jew, as a man, is usually quite up to the average degree of physical fitness, but the Russian Jews by the deliberate neglect of every species of physical exercise and by means of an absolute determination to become weak, manage to get themselves rejected as soldiers, in numbers out of all proportion to the relative size of their community.

ARTHUR SAXON [1878-1921].

Mentioned in this very work as "the best lifter of his time," he is widely regarded as the favorite and most accomplished strongman of his era.

A figure of inspiration for many others, this strongman still holds world and historical records in lifts such as the bent press and the two-hands-anyhow. His life has been thoroughly analyzed in my compilation, "Arthur Saxon: The Book of Weightlifting", authored by Jerónimo Milo and based on Saxon's famous 1908 book.

This is the first volume in the "Masters of Strength" series, part of the larger collection of books and manuals, which also includes "The Way to Live".

"Wer will kann" (he who has the will has the power) was the motto of Herr Unthan, the man without arms, who succeeded in developing his feet in such a manner that he could use them to better advantage than many a clever man can use his hands. Another similar case is the one of Miss Rapin, the clever Swiss painter and artist, who was born without arms. My readers probably know of numerous similar cases. Again, I have come across many young men, who by nature seemed very weak, but who, in consequence of physical exercises and a strong will power, became prominently strong.

You must have faith in your ability to make yourself strong. It has already been proved at the present day that thought constitutes real power. A very clever apparatus has been invented, and is in existence, called the "muscle bed". This automatically registers which parts of the body are provided with a more liberal flow of blood, by the simple impulse, will or thought of the person measured. Consequently, it is by no means immaterial how and what one thinks. Banish,

HACK SQUAT

This particular squat is performed with the feet supported on the area of the phalanges and metatarsals, while lifting the heels and pointing the toes diagonally outward. It resembles an old-style deep knee bend but with the load hanging behind the body, which also stimulates the anterior core.

The hack squat is attributed to Hackenschmidt, as he not only popularized it but also shares his name with it. However, the term "hack" actually originates from the German word "hacke", meaning "hoe", referring to the tool used for working the soil.

therefore, all your sad or miserable thoughts, and keep on with your physical training, without ever thinking for one moment that you might not succeed.

GOVERN YOUR THOUGHTS

This rule is absolutely necessary in all stages of life if you wish to succeed, for without concentration of thought, you are courting failure. How many people are there who are, so to speak, the shuttlecock of their thoughts! Every moment hundreds of ideas or thoughts rush through their brain, causing an expenditure of energy without adequate return in results. Just fancy a man at the Bisley rifle range taking aim and shooting at the same moment as he thinks of something quite different. Do you think he will carry off the King's prize, or, indeed, any prize? No, he will not even hit the target. If, therefore, you wish to become healthy and strong, you must give your thoughts to the full and without restriction in this direction, even to the most insignificant performances of your daily life. Concentrate your mind upon the idea of acquiring health and strength!

To give a few examples. The ordinary mortal may be reading his daily paper or book while taking his meals; his mind is occupied with what he is reading, instead of being bent on acquiring nourishment. He neglects proper mastication of his food, hence arise—indigestion, non-assimilation of food, bad teeth, and other ailments. Many people who suffered from painful chronic indigestion have been cured of it by the simple remedy, however strange it sounds: thorough mastication. Another man will train for years according to a fairly good method, but he neglects to devote his mind to his movements. Instead of clin-ging to the one important thought, "I will become strong", or "I will strengthen this particular muscle", he allows his thoughts to be distracted from the main point; the result is useless training, simply manual labour without increase of strength, but, perhaps, decrease. Every wrestler will admit that thoughts are powers; whilst one is measuring one's strength and skill with an opponent, one's thoughts must be concentrated on the game, otherwise defeat is certain. A wrestler whose attention or thought is distracted invariably loses.

As I mentioned before, it has been proved by experiments that thought can influence a livelier rush of blood to certain parts of the body, hence the hot head and cold feet of the brain worker.

A physical culture pupil will profit by this knowledge, and avoid, for instance, erotic thoughts, for he who has erotic thoughts steers his blood into organs which are superfluous for our purpose, instead of into the arms and legs, which he intends to, and should, make strong.

BETWEEN CONSERVATIVE AND PROGRESSIVE

During Hackenschmidt's era, sports and physical activity were beginning to gain widespread acceptance. In Great Britain, physical culture was seen as a means to organize a disciplined and orderly society. The emerging ideal portrayed the body as a temple of health and purity, heavily influenced by the military and Christian values of the time.

Among the "recommendations" found in many texts of that era, there was frequent advice calling for moderation in various aspects of social life, particularly concerning sexual activity. It's no surprise that suggestions about sexual activity in relation to training performance appeared frequently.

Over time, research has shown no evidence of any decline or risks to performance, yet these notions persist in the collective subconscious.

Ironically, as this "purification" movement evolved, the strongman world of the time provided a space where nudity was accepted. In some cases, clubs, theaters, and "special" photography sessions became the only venues where alternative forms of sexual expression could be explored—expressions that would have been neither presented nor accepted elsewhere during that period.

One ought to avoid all unnecessary worry and exciting thoughts, and to cultivate a firm tranquillity of mind. I have formed the conviction that all unnecessary sorrows and cares act in all circumstances harmfully upon one's constitution. Melancholy reflections will in no way influence Fate, whereas one may weaken the constitution by the waste of energy while indulging in them. The best is to do one's duty conscientiously, and to leave the rest to Him who guides our destiny.

"No one is ever too old to start exercising".

He who wants to become strong can succeed in conquering his failings and mastering his shortcomings by regulating his life accordingly.

Under this heading I would include the consumption of alcohols and tobacco, coffee, etc. Alcohol is, in my opinion, a nerve poison, which is not assimilated and requires a great expenditure of energy for its excretion. Furthermore, it decreases energy and deadens certain inner forces, of which we may be unconscious and which otherwise may be of great service to us. For instance, we may be tired, that is, our senses bid us leave off and rest, and thus collect fresh natural energy. But under the influence of alcohol, we are easily induced to act against our natural instinct, and as each action is followed by a reaction, the latter shows itself in various disagreeable and eventually harmful shapes: depression of spirit, bad humour, bad digestion, loss of appetite, and so forth. Alcohol, therefore, or any similar stimulant which has an unnatural effect, must be injurious.

MINERVA

Hamburg, Germany [1865-1923]

Minerva was one of the most successful strongwomen in history. She began her journey in artistic gymnastics at the age of 7 and started lifting weights at a very young age. By 11, she was already training with 35 kg dumbbells.
Minerva did not limit herself to theatrical feats of strength; with a 300 kg deadlift and a one-hand press of 45 kg, she demonstrated extraordinary power. She became the first Women's World Wrestling Champion during the late 19th century.

The consumption of tobacco is the most useless vice which exists. Nicotine is a direct poison to the heart, and, like alcohol, is very harmful.

I will admit that I can see no crime in an occasional indulgence in a glass of wine or a cigar; the main point is simply to be able to keep one's body and mind under full control. You may compare the connection of body and mind or soul to that between the mesmerist and his medium. It is a well-known fact that the oftener the medium submits to the will of the mesmerist the more easily the state of hypnotism is reached. If, therefore, the mind or soul submits to the suggestions of the weaker organ, the body, which bids him to have a smoke now and again, to neglect physical exercise today, or to indulge to excess for once in alcoholic drink, the morrow will repeat this suggestion with easier and possibly increased success. Hence, to obey your body weakens the will, whilst to control it gives one strength of mind.

Moderation in sexual intercourse is very important. Sexual abstemiousness should be strictly observed during the early age of manhood and development. He who observes this recommendation will soon benefit by the immense prerogatives of chastity. A few years ago a colleague of mine said to me: "Nonsense, that is only human nature". This "clever" man, however, reached only a secondary position as a strong man, and now, at the age of thirty, he is actually degenerating as an athlete. Coffee is a stimulant and, as such, would be better avoided entirely.

CHAPTER V

Nutrition.

I come now to the much-discussed subject:

WHAT OUGHT WE TO EAT?

I believe I am right in asserting that our Creator has provided food and nutriment for every being for its own advantage. Man is born without frying-pan or stewpot. The purest natural food for human beings would, therefore, be fresh, uncooked food and nuts. It is not my intention to discuss here the old problem, whether meat is necessary as food for man or whether man was created and should remain a vegetarian. My experience has taught me that foodstuffs are of secondary importance. There are very strong people who are strict vegetarians, whilst others eat a good deal of meat. A fare which consists of three-quarters of vegetable food and one-quarter meat would appear to be the most satisfactory for the people of central Europe.

Every one should and can find out which diet best suits his constitution, and he should avoid all food which disagrees with it. I would shun altogether all highly seasoned and sour dishes. Much has been said lately in praise of sugar as food, but as artificial sugar is an acid-forming substance, I should not recommend it. Natural sugar, such as is contained in dates, figs, and other fruit, is certainly preferable. Highly flavoured or seasoned food produces thirst and therefore acts harmfully.

HOW MUCH SHOULD WE EAT?

I maintain that it is absolutely a mistake to eat a great deal, Excess is harmful, as all food which the stomach only partly digests, transforms itself in the stomach or in the intestines into poisonous matter, which in time sets up bodily decay. It is true that to a certain extent digestion improves as muscle strength increases, but even in such cases the progress may not be sufficient for a thorough assimilation of the extra food.

The disadvantages of meat foods are, in my opinion, in the first place, that nowadays it is most difficult to obtain meat from absolutely healthy animals (I count those artificially fed in stables and pens among the unhealthy ones), and secondly, that far too much flesh food is taken.

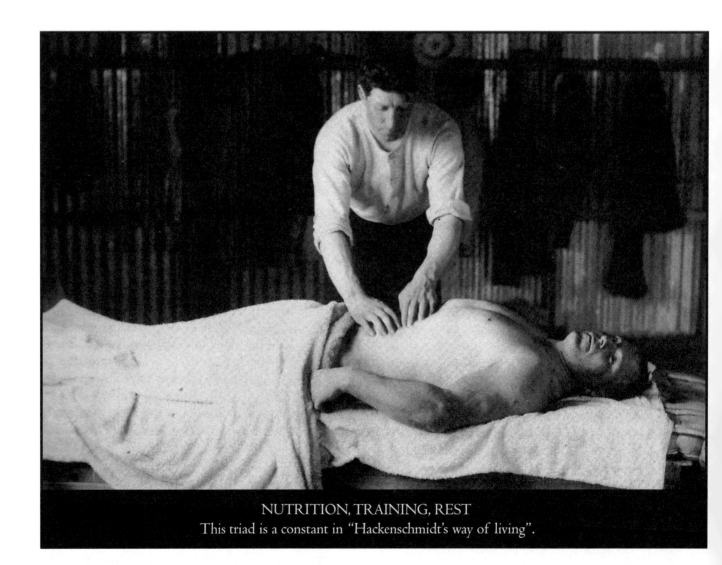

NUTRITION, TRAINING, REST
This triad is a constant in "Hackenschmidt's way of living".

In the case of pure vegetable food, excess is less dangerous. All food, with perhaps the exception of pure vegetables, which certainly form the ideal human food, deposits drossy sediments in the body, which may be removed by four channels, the lungs, the skin, the kidneys, and the intestines. If these four channels are in good working order, the man is healthy.

THE ETERNAL TOPIC OF DIETS

Perhaps the most discussed topic accompanying every manual, book, class, post, and advertisement over the past 150 years is: what and how much to eat when committing to structured training.

Even today, this subject continues to spark conflicting opinions and physiological justifications among advocates of various nutritional habits. Hackenschmidt emphasizes WHAT and HOW MUCH, effectively addressing questions people still search for on Google more than a century later.

Regarding these eternal debates, Hackenschmidt offers an interesting perspective on meat—not focusing so much on the food itself but on its source. He was already concerned about animals raised on artificial feed and the conditions in which they were kept in captivity. He acknowledges that the discussion about meat is "ancient," giving us insight into how long this issue has been debated in human history. From his experience, he notes that being vegetarian should not necessarily affect performance in training.

Another notable point is his belief that muscle strength improves digestion, aligning with modern concepts (like osteopathic approaches) that link the structures of the musculoskeletal system with digestive function.

Without being an expert or having access to today's information, Hackenschmidt made an insightful statement on this topic:
"Each person must and can find the diet that best suits their constitution and avoid any food that disagrees with it."

This is one of his most compelling assertions, as it highlights the importance of individuality and cautions against generalizing in a topic with so many nuances.

THE PRINCIPAL FOOD FOR MAN IS THE PURE AIR.

Partake of it as much as you possibly can, breathe much, and as deeply as you can, through the nose. Breathing through the nose is the only proper way of respiration and at the same time an important regulator for the movement of the body, for, if for any kind of work the breath through the nose ceases to be sufficient, one ought to either discontinue the work or restrict the movement until breathing has again become normal.

Various deep-breathing exercises are recommended by professors and other so-called authorities on Physical Culture matters. Not wishing to be dragged into any discussion I will refrain from criticising these, and will confine myself to strongly recommending all my readers to content themselves with the simplest and most natural deep-breathing exercise in existence. One which every one can practise, without trouble, and which requires no argument to demonstrate its superiority over all others.

This consists simply of running exercise in the open air. Run as much as you can and as often as you can, and whenever you come across a hill, run up it. This will force you to inhale deep breaths and will also accustom you to breathe through your nose. Besides the chest and lung development resulting therefrom, you will soon appreciate the benefits which your leg muscles will derive. I cannot lay too great stress upon the great usefulness of proper breathing, by which means we introduce into our system the essential oxygen and discharge a quantity of waste matter.

The skin of most people is in a very neglected state. In consequence of unsuitable clothing or imperfect cleansing of the countless pores, the poisonous residues cannot be expelled through the skin. These impurities consequently accumulate in the region of other outlets, such as the kidneys; if these are in good order, the function intended for the skin may be in part performed by them, but if this state of things continues, kidney disorders are sure to appear, just as skin disease will come

HEINRICH "MILO" STEINBORN

Siegburg, Germany [1894–1989]

As a child, Henry Steinborn began his athletic journey as a gymnast and later worked as a merchant sailor during his teenage years. When World War I began, he was captured as a German and sent to a prisoner-of-war camp. This was where he had his first encounter with weightlifting, as prisoners practiced exercises using homemade bars and construction blocks.

In 1921, seeking a better life and opportunities, Steinborn emigrated to the United States and settled in Philadelphia. There, he launched his professional career as a strongman and quickly gained recognition in the circuit. That same year, Steinborn broke three world records: the squat, the one-hand snatch, and the continental lift.

It was during this time that he met Alan Calvert, the founder of Milo Barbell Company, the leading producer of weightlifting equipment in the United States at the time. Stein-

born famously broke the squat record by lifting 250 kg without the use of a rack.

Undoubtedly, Henry Steinborn was the man who popularized the squat in the United States, transforming it into a cornerstone of modern physical culture.

if the kidneys and intestines work badly, and then the patient generally and foolishly tries to cure or improve the skin with salves or cosmetics.

For these reasons it must be obvious that running is a far more satisfactory breathing exercise than the mere filling and emptying of the lungs before an open window, the accompanying exertion compelling the discharge of these impurities in the form of respiration. An important item of physical culture, indeed, is a regular care of the skin. One or two weekly baths and daily rubbing of the whole body are necessary. As to the temperature of the water, you must use your own judgment. He who dives into cold water or takes a cold douche when he is hot, or perspiring, suppresses forcibly the action of the pores and exposes himself to illness. As we are all more or less the opposite to hardy, such violent attempts at "hardening ourselves" act detrimentally on our health. Swimming is very useful, but I should not advise a longer stay in the water than one quarter of an hour at a time, as the temperature of the body becomes so low that a great amount of energy has to be expended specially to raise the warmth of the body again.

When training, a cold morning bath of one half to one minute's duration before commencing will be found very beneficial. If at all possible, expose the naked body to the sun. Man is a creature of light and air, and I should therefore recommend little or no clothing when training.

WHAT WE SHOULD DRINK.

In this, excess is also prejudicial, first, because one gives the kidneys more work than they were intended for, and, secondly, the very important mineral salts which the body requires for nourishment are carried away by the extra liquid. According to the discoveries of the German, Julius Hensel, it is just the presence in the body of these mineral salts, such as iron, lime, sodium, phosphorus, sulphur, chlorides and bromides, which supports energy and vital power, and if they are wanting, decay of tissue and decomposition take place. The invigorating action of salt air is partly due to the copious amount of salts and mineral matter it contains.

A German proverb says rightly: "He who drinks and has no thirst, Or who eats and has no hunger, Unlike him whose health is first, Suffers illness and dies younger."

It is said that a large percentage of America's population suffers from weak or diseased stomachs through partaking of highly seasoned foods, or from kidney complaints through indulgence in iced drinks. It is very unwise to drink anything cold if one's body is overheated; one ought to take small mouthfuls, and swallow each only after having warmed it in one's mouth. I need not occupy space in dilating on the well-known pernicious effect of too hot liquids upon teeth and stomach.

HACK PREDICTED IT

In this manual, besides discussing training for athletes and wrestlers, Hackenschmidt takes the time to address training for the "common" person, struggling with the demands of daily work. He recognized that training was not merely a vehicle for improving wrestling or strength but also a tool for the everyday man and woman working in sedentary jobs. He advocated for the benefits of training not only for the musculoskeletal system but also for the "efficiency of the heart, stomach, lungs, intestines, liver, and other organs." He already viewed health as a comprehensive set of abilities that needed to be stimulated and developed.

His most emphatic statement almost reads like a warning that no one would dare ignore: "Those who choose not to engage in some form of physical exercise will be unable to prevent their muscles and nervous system from experiencing the kind of self-poisoning known as atrophy."

This statement leads us to question whether the sedentarism, obesity, and other societal ailments we face today were already emerging in Hackenschmidt's time, and if he managed to perceive them as a significant threat to society.

This perspective also explains the comprehensiveness of the manual under analysis. It includes joint mobility training, stretching of soft tissues, and structural and tension work specific to the muscles. In addition, it incorporates recommendations for rest, nutrition, and outdoor activities (similar to those in *Arthur Saxon's book, albeit with perhaps less physiological grounding), making the training applicable to all aspects of daily life.

CHAPTER VI

Rest and wholesome sleep

The natural invigorating remedy for an exhausted body is rest, both in the physical and mental direction, and a healthy sleep. This is the only means by which the various organs and muscles may rid themselves of the "fatigue poison" and collect and develop fresh energy. I have already touched on the necessity of controlling one's thoughts and the method of doing so, and would now refer to a few dispositions of mind which are very detrimental; these are excitement, worry, fretting, and anger. Avoid violent emotion, also gambling, worry about unavoidable or unalterable situations, etc. All these emotions draw blood into the brain and thus cause a weakening of the other organs used for work and movement. Be careful in the choice of literature. Here also avoid excess, and especially erotic novels.

To obtain a sound sleep, the regulation of the proper functions of the intestines and the skin is necessary above everything else.

He who takes daily and thorough exercise in the open will hardly be plagued by sleeplessness. It is advisable to observe as far as possible regular hours for sleep. Sleep during the night is better than during daytime. Seven to nine hours suffice amply, and here again too much is unwholesome. Nervous people, or those who work much with the brain, would do well to rest once or twice a day for about one quarter to half an hour after a meal.

DWELLING ROOMS

Unhealthy dwelling rooms are very injurious. Bedrooms, in particular, should be well-ventilated and exposed to sunlight. I should recommend every father of a family to arrange his dwelling so that the largest and best-situated rooms are used as bedrooms, seeing that one-third of one's life is spent there. Damp walls, damp bedclothes, and the like are to be rigorously avoided, and care in this direction cannot be too greatly insisted upon. The least evils which they bring are gout, rheumatism, colds, etc.

Heavy curtains in bedrooms should be avoided, also large carpets, which cannot easily be cleaned. Both harbour dust and impurities. Small curtains should frequently be washed.

CLOTHING

Clothes should not be too warm nor too tight, in order to allow free action to the function of the skin, and to the development of the several parts of the body. Corsets and tight boots are no good for a physical culturist. A very good material for clothing, if it were not too dear, is silk; after this comes good linen (most suitable for underwear), wool, and cotton.

RECOMMENDATIONS FOR A GOOD LIFE

Like a modern influencer, Hackenschmidt had already grasped the public's desire to be told what to eat, how to train, how to rest, and, in other words, how to live. Hack makes it clear that not everyone will be willing to follow "George Hackenschmidt's Way of Living". In this clever marketing phrase, we can see how he employed an effective reverse psychology strategy, akin to "this isn't for everyone", "not everyone can handle this", or "this is only for a select group". A tactic reminiscent of how CrossFit attracted more followers in the past decade.

"Those who choose not to commit to some form of regular exercise cannot prevent their nervous and muscular systems from experiencing a form of self-poisoning known as ATROPHY". With this brilliant and metaphorical description, Hack refers to the effects of sedentarism, which he labels as a form of "self-poisoning". His words perfectly align with one of today's most pervasive plagues: prolonged exposure to computers, chairs, and artificial lighting, all of which penalize our musculoskeletal system, subjecting it to a constant and progressive state of decay and atrophy.

Hackenschmidt had already observed that modern life—offices, repetitive manual labor in unhealthy conditions—would become one of the "poisons" plaguing human health. He believed that one of the solutions to combat this was exercise and, more specifically, strength development. Some of his more outdated suggestions, such as "avoiding erotic thoughts," might align more with the moral standards of his time.

While subjective and personal models often don't apply universally, Hack's "way of living" worked perfectly for him, allowing him to maintain strength and agility until the age of 91.

I have now made mention of the principal items which act beneficially or detrimentally upon the physical development of man, among which there are many recommendations with which the reader is no doubt familiar, but which cannot be repeated too often. I admit that these counsels may seem superfluous to some, but their careful observance will help one not only to keep well but to gain the physical strength which I believe to be the goal of my readers.

I have come across all sorts and conditions of people among the many who have asked my advice or opinion on different subjects, and on my own principles for the attainment of the strength and muscular development which gained for me such reputation as I may possess, either as a wrestler or as an athlete.

I have seen would-be athletes who cared most for the exterior of their bodies, and others who were faddists or cranks; these people would try all sorts of novelties in dress, diet, apparatus, food, etc. They fell from one extreme into the other, and believed that they could become strong by easy and comfortable means, forgetting that there are only two principal means of acquiring strength—exercise and perseverance.

MISS LALA

Szczecin, Kingdom of Prussia (modern-day Poland) [1858-1919?].

Olga Brown, better known as "Miss Lala", was a circus performer born to a German father and a French mother of African descent. She began her circus career at the age of 9, specializing in acts of balance, strength, and danger. Lala was renowned for her "Iron Jaw" stunts, using her mouth and teeth to climb ropes and suspend herself at great heights. Edmond Desbonnet mentions her in his 1911 book "The Kings of Strength", where he praises her astonishing strength and exceptional physique. She was immortalized by Impressionist painter Edgar Degas in his 1879 artwork, "Miss Lala at the Cirque Fernand".

CHAPTER VII
Training

BEFORE I describe what I consider the best method of training for the acquisition of strength, I should like to make a few remarks with regard to its application. It stands to reason that the natural bent and abilities for physical development in different people vary with the individual. An old man will have to train differently from a young man, a woman differently from a child, while there are various gradations for age and sex. There are, however, a great many people who seem to be hindered by their vocation or calling from a methodical training on these lines. To these I would say that there is always some time available every day which can be devoted to physical exercises and the care of the body. If you wish to become strong and well, you must attend to this, just as you must find time for eating. And, again, if you do not find time to become and remain healthy, you will be obliged to find time to be ill. Surely some of the hours wasted on banal and often harmful pleasures might be devoted to physical exercise.

Of course, I am aware that there are people whose occupation is very trying, and others who undergo great mental strain. I should recommend such to study and follow particularly the part of my book dealing with the mastery and concentration of thought while they are training, when their success will be certain. Brain workers must, however, proceed with particular care following the maxim, "Slowly but surely". They will require months where others require weeks owing to their more favourable conditions; but the result will be the same.

THE BEST METHOD OF TRAINING

As a principal rule I should stipulate for regularity of training. Any observant student will have noticed that the mechanism of the body reacts uncons-ciously, and with an often surprising punctuality, consequent upon certain repeated activity, by reason of its habit and adaptability. For instance, if one follows a regular mode of life, one wakens always at the same hour; hunger and vigour, etc., are also similarly experienced at certain times of the day. Hence it is advisable to exercise as nearly as possible at the same hour every day. The time will, of course, vary with different people. I should not advise the practice of physical exercise, more particularly exercise with weights, in the morning immediately after rising, as most people are not then particularly vigorous. The best time is during the two hours previous or subsequent to a principal meal; if before, one ought to leave off at least a quarter of an hour before eating, so that the nerves may become calm, otherwise loss of appetite may be entailed.

The exercises should not exceed one quarter of an hour at the commencement, and should only be increased by five minutes in a few months. Afterwards, about thirty minutes are fully sufficient for the acquisition and preservation of strength and endurance.

Another useful point to notice is that it is unadvisable to sit down and rest between the exercises, as not only is one likely to contract a chill by so doing, but the muscles themselves will become stiff and contracted. You will naturally be wearing a minimum of clothing while exercising, so as soon as you have run through one series, throw a towel or wrap over your shoulders and walk briskly up and down the room. This will keep the blood circulating and rebuilding the consumed tissue. It will also assist the process of perspiration or discharge of waste matter, and will above all assist in the maintenance of looseness and suppleness in joint, muscle and sinew so highly to be desired by the athlete whose ambition is directed towards the acquisition of health and strength and not merely that development which is intended to display itself solely before a looking glass or camera.

All exercises should be made slowly, and with full concentration of the mind; observe by all means regular breathing, carefully waiting after every exercise until a calm respiration through the nose has again taken place.

There are certain advantages in going through the exercises with one or two companions, but if these are mere spectators, it is better to exercise alone, for fear of having one's thoughts diverted from the work.

CHARMION

Sacramento, United States [1875-1949].

Laverie Vallée, known by her stage name "Charmion," was an American trapeze artist famous for her performances that showcased her impressive strength and muscular physique, all while performing a provocative striptease on the trapeze. Her act was part of a wave of early 20th-century female trapeze artists who defied the "Victorian" values of the era.

Charmion was among the first women to leverage the burgeoning fields of photography and cinema to promote her performances, even appearing in the early films of Thomas Edison. Her shows embodied both the fears and desires of contemporary society, challenging societal norms and sparking reflection on accepted ideals of sexuality, physical fitness, and the female body at the time.

VARIATIONS IN THE EXERCISES

It is advisable to vary the exercises constantly, so as to avoid too great a strain on single muscle groups, and rather to develop all muscles harmoniously.

I should like to point here to a great mistake which a vast number of thoughtless people make during training. Every human being has a certain part of his body more developed by nature than other parts; say, for instance, that the legs of one or the arms of another are naturally strong. Now, the former will be able to perform the leg exercises with perfect ease and comfort, whereas all his arm exercises require more exertion. It would be foolish if this particular individual were to devote more time and attention to his leg exercises because they are easier to him, and neglect his arm exercises, which to him are harder and more difficult. Nevertheless, this is a bad habit into which many people fall during training. While in this case the legs become stronger, the arms do not develop in the same ratio. It is, therefore, most necessary to train systematically.

Further on I shall give particulars of the various exercises, and I recommend my readers to map out a certain plan, according to which they exercise all the muscle groups twice on three or four days every week, or on six days, if time allows.

"Over time, everyone will come to recognize the importance of performing physical exercises daily, in one form or another, as a regular counterbalance to the mental effort of daily life."

CHAPTER VIII

Exercises without weights

I can hear a few of my readers exclaiming, "These instructions are all, no doubt, excellent, but then I am not going to exercise with weights. My doctor doesn't approve of them for one thing, and I myself am not particularly keen on them for another. Besides which I travel about a good deal, attending to my business, and it would be highly inconvenient for me to have to add bar-bells, dumb-bells, etc., to my ordinary luggage".

In response to these objections, I can only say that the last one raised does certainly possess a certain amount of force, although by purchasing a series of disc weights, the encumbrance would be reduced to a minimum in the matters of weight, bulk, and cost.

As to the others, well, it is my opinion that everyone—man, woman, and child without exception—will find exercise with a graduated and suitably adapted series of weights of the utmost benefit. Nevertheless, I do not expect everyone to be converted to my views, however convinced I may personally be of their merit. As to medical views on the matter, well, I have had the pleasure of hearing the opinions of every leading medical authority in the world who has really studied the matter, and they are, one and all, in agreement with those which I myself entertain and have set forth in these pages.

Medical men who are opposed to exercises with weights have never investigated them, and are totally ignorant of their value. No living person is so weak as to be unable to exercise in this fashion, all that is necessary being to graduate the weights. Even a weak heart can be strengthened by exercises with weights.

Still, I am aware there are certain people who may entertain a sentimental objection to strength and who object, in consequence, to run any risk of acquiring a powerful muscular development. All these people are, however, anxious to preserve their own health and to avoid any necessity of incurring expense in the shape of medical attendance and drugs. As already pointed out, health cannot be divorced from strength. The body, in order to be healthy, must be strong, so that it will be found that the series of exercises set forth in this chapter, while being free from all inconvenient possibilities of great strength development, will yet, if conscientiously practised, develop a fair average physique, as well as a sound, all-round physical fitness—in other words, a sound and healthy constitution.

There is one other reason for this chapter, or rather for the exercises detailed therein, being deserving of especial attention, and that is that these exercises without weights should be regarded as being a preliminary course even for those ambitious of athletic renown.

Even where a youth is so naturally strong and fit that he might safely enter straight away on a course of weight-lifting exercises, and of exercises with

A WELL-STRUCTURED METHOD

It's remarkable to see such an intelligent, progressive, and organized approach in a manual from so long ago.

Hack begins by emphasizing the importance of precautions and safeguards before embarking on a training method. He carefully considers the needs of individuals with prior injuries as well as the necessary care for special populations.
The method then introduces a structured and progressive series of mobility exercises, combined with isometrics and balance-focused movements, aimed at addressing muscular tension imbalances—what he

refers to as "unloaded exercises".

Only after establishing a solid foundation of mobility, balance, and optimal muscle tension does Hack encourage the practice of basic weight exercises in the following chapter. These exercises are designed to stimulate muscle groups and specific movement patterns.

With this foundation in place, one can finally progress to classical barbell lifts, many of which are performed with "one hand", presenting the ultimate challenge for stabilization and unilateral strength.

weights, he will be well advised if he devotes at least two or three weeks to these exercises without weights, and further to include a fair selection of them in his programme of daily exercise with weights. I have myself repeated a few in my next chapter, partly as an indication of the method I would like my readers to follow, and while the ones I have repeated must on no account be neglected, I would not wish anyone to think that on this account the others may be passed over altogether.

The exercises themselves will be found to include movements which will strengthen every necessary part of the human frame, and should therefore be patronized in ratio to the actual need for same; i.e., a reader suffering or liable to attacks of indigestion, constipation or other intestinal disorders, should pay particular attention to Exercises 6, 8, 9, 10, and 13; while a reader in need of chest, neck, and throat development would, on the other hand, rely mainly on Exercises 1, 2, 3, 4, 5, and 14. Sufficient indications, however, are given with the exercises themselves to enable anyone to make his or her own selection.

ERNEST CADINE

París, France [1893-1978]

He was a French weightlifter and Olympic gold medalist in weightlifting at the 1920 Antwerp Olympics.

From a young age, he trained in various sports, including artistic gymnastics, Greco-Roman wrestling, weightlifting, and swimming.

Between 1920 and 1925, he set six world records, including a 140 kg Clean & Jerk and a 108 kg Snatch.
After retiring from his athletic career, he became a successful professional strongman.

I would, however, strongly advise one and all to pay full attention to the advice already given on the subjects of Nutrition, Rest, Breathing Exercises, etc., and to adhere as closely as possible to the lines previously laid down with regard to these points. I would also like to see a fair amount of attention paid to the exercises dealt with in Chapter IX. They may not care to carry these out with the weights recommended therewith, perhaps, but there are some, notably those for neck development, chest development, strengthening the abdominal muscles, etc., which should on no account be neglected.

The weights utilized for these could be, if necessary, considerably reduced, say to a half, or even less, of the minimum advised. This will, and indeed should, depend almost entirely on the physical powers of the reader himself. I cannot

CHARLES RIGOULOT

Le Vesinet, France. [1903-1962].

He was a French weightlifter, professional wrestler, racecar driver, and actor.
He began training with weights as a child and was lifting heavy loads by the age of 16. As a weightlifter, he won a gold medal in the under 82 kg division at the 1924 Paris Olympics. Throughout the 1920s, he broke numerous records and is considered to have performed "the best one-handed snatch in the world". In 1930, he became the first person to lift the "Apollon's Wheel" overhead [page 31]. In 1932, he transitioned to a career as a professional strongman in various circuses, also performing and singing in theatrical productions. Years later, he became a racecar driver, competing in the renowned Le Mans race in 1937.

pretend to be acquainted with those of each and every one. In order to institute a scale, it is only necessary to remember that the weights prescribed (save in the section for athletes) are well within the normal healthy and active man's powers, and that ladies and children, elderly and invalid readers must, to a large extent, fix the amount most suitable to themselves by an estimate formed on that basis; and, further, in making such decision, that it will be safer to under-estimate rather than over-estimate their own strength to commence with.

I would suggest that at least fifteen minutes be daily devoted to the system of exercises adopted, the best period being immediately after rising, subsequent to the matutinal bath.

As an alternative to the above, nightly exercise, i.e., just before retiring, is almost as good, and in certain cases (when one does not sleep well, for instance) even preferable.

Never on any account continue the exercises until exhaustion sets in and always relax your muscles afterwards, in the manner recommended in the last chapter. Further, do not devote your whole attention solely to the easiest movements. These will very probably be calculated to develop those parts in which you are already strong, whereas your chief aim should be to so strengthen your less well-developed muscles, that your body may be in perfect harmony and tune.

Look upon this condition as being the goal of your ambitions, concentrate your thoughts thereon and on the muscles which your exercise is developing, thereby assisting your progress.

TO INVALIDS AND LEISURED PERSONS

I would specially offer the recommendation that they devote several quarters of an hour daily to the practice of the majority of the exercises dealt with in this chapter. By so doing they will (if ill) be hastening their recovery and fortifying their systems against future attacks of illness, and all such will, in any case, be profitably employing hours which might otherwise hang somewhat heavily on their hands.

MIDDLE-AGED AND ELDERLY PEOPLE

Middle-aged and elderly people are far too apt to imagine that for them the age of physical exercise is past. Herein they are really seriously at fault, for they are often the very people who stand most in need of such. They, for instance, are the ones most liable to suffer from superfluous adipose tissue, defective digestion, and irregular circulation. They would indeed benefit considerably by the exercises detailed in Chapter IX, but as (supposing them to be commencing exercise for the first time) they will possibly shrink from the use of dumb-bells and bar-bells, I have perhaps borne them more in mind while arranging the following series. As far as possible, therefore, should they devote their attention to these, and as soon as their interest has been sufficiently awakened enter upon the advanced course, under, of course, lighter conditions than those recommended for younger readers, with the less strenuous movements, persevering with these until they are able practically to run through the whole series.

SPECIAL AUDIENCE

Hack dedicates a section to what he refers to as the "special audience": older adults, individuals with disabilities, or those considered "inactive". He recommends several 15-minute daily training blocks, focusing initially on sequences of bodyweight exercises before progressing to those involving weights. He also emphasizes the importance of adjusting both the weights and repetitions to suit individual needs.

"Older people who tend to think that their time for exercise has passed... are often the ones who need it the most", Hack declares, addressing a pervasive misconception deeply rooted in modern society: "The older we are, the less sense it makes to start training."

Quite the opposite should be true! It is widely known that after the age of 40, humans begin to lose approximately 1% of muscle mass per year, making strength training essential.

Not only does strength training help maintain muscle mass and strength levels—thereby preventing hormonal imbalances—but it also combats excess body fat, poor digestion, and irregular circulation.

No. I   Stand erect with hands clasped behind your neck. Now press the head forcibly down until the chin touches the chest, exerting the full strength of your neck muscles to resist the pressure. When the chin is down, force the head back by exertion of the neck muscles against the hand pressure. Repeat this alternate movement, at first for five repetitions, gradually increasing same. Neck muscles specially.

No. 2- Stand erect and roll the head round and round by bending the neck in a circular motion. Continue for, say, ten repetitions, gradually increasing the number up to twenty. Neck muscles specially.

No. 3- Stand erect with elbows at sides, arms bent at right angles, hands clenched. Now roll your shoulders right round if possible: back, up, forward, and down. Continue until tired. Shoulder muscles specially.

No. 4- Stand erect with arms stretched straight out in front of you, palms turned inwards. Force arms straight back into line with the shoulders. Raise them sideways to full stretch above head, palms facing to the front, and bring them down in front of you at full stretch, till the palms rest on the front of the thighs. Return to full stretch above head and then to the first position. Continue exercise for, say, a full minute. Chest expansion mainly.

No. 5- Stand with right leg crossed over left, both arms crossed across chest, hands clasping shoulders. Spring out to a full stride of each leg sideways, throwing arms back, hands open, to a line with the shoulders. Return sharply and continue for twenty repetitions. All leg muscles, as well as the arms, shoulders, back, and chest will be greatly benefited.

No. 6- Stand erect with feet close together, arms and hands fully stretched above the head. Now swing the trunk right round in a circular motion (as near as possible), bending over to the right, forward, round to the left, and back, waist circling or swinging from the hips only. Continue for five to ten full circles at first, according to the ease with which the movement can be executed, and increase gradually. Persevere until tired, but not as far as exhaustion. Keep arms loose. This exercise will be found specially helpful in cases of intestinal disorder, particularly when accompanied by a too extensive waist. The spine will also be considerably strengthened.

EXERCISES FOR THE ORGANS?

The idea that physical training can enhance the structure and function of internal organs is not entirely "new." Historical references to this concept can be found in ancient practices like Chinese Qi Gong methods, including the "Eight Pieces of Brocade", "Muscle and Tendon Transformation", and "Bone Marrow Cleansing",
What is particularly fascinating is that, centuries later, someone like Hackenschmidt—completely removed from these cultures and practices—arrived at similar conclusions through purely empirical observation.

These ideas also align with modern concepts seen in visceral osteopathy, which suggests that all structures in the body are interconnected, either through direct connections (fascia, ligaments, or tissues) or functional relationships (circulation, drainage, hormonal stimulation).

This makes the concept that physical training could influence the form and function of an organ not only holistic but also remarkably forward-thinking for its time.

No. 7- Stand erect, feet together, arms fully stretched, palms of hands pressed together. Then, keeping all muscles taut, bend down carefully, elevating the left leg into such a position as would enable a straight line to be drawn along the back of the hands to the extended heel. Endeavour to approach as closely to this position as it is possible to assume—the knee of the supporting leg may be slightly bent if necessary to get as near to the desired result as possible. Go slowly back and repeat forward bend, extending right leg. Continue for five repetitions, increasing one per week to twenty repetitions. Highly developing all the leg muscles. The arms, hip, back, and shoulders will also derive great benefit, particularly in the extensor muscles. Its influence on height may readily be observed.

No. 8- Stand erect, feet together, arms fully stretched, palms facing each other. Bend right forward from the hips as far down as possible without bending the knees, and then swing right back as far as possible. Repeat five times each movement alternately, increasing gradually to twenty repetitions. Abdominal and back muscles.

No. 9- Lie down full length on floor as shown in sketch and raise the legs to right angles with the body. Repeat five times and increase gradually, say by one repetition a week. Abdominal, back, and hip muscles.

No. 10- Lie down full length as shown and rise into sitting posture without moving the legs. This may at first necessitate a counterpoise of some sort, such as hooking the feet under a chest of drawers or something of the kind, but persevere until you can rise without any such assistance. Repeat five times and increase gradually as last. Similar muscles affected, but in slightly different manner and proportion.

THIS TYPE OF TRAINING?

It might seem curious that in a book about strength, which also extensively covers wrestling, so many mobility exercises are included—some of which might even appear outdated. However, don't be misled; upon closer analysis, these exercises serve as an excellent precursor to strength training and specific physical preparation for wrestling movements.

At first glance, this may resemble old-fashioned "calisthenics," but these exercises strike a fine balance between strength and mobility for the body parts involved in more complex movements. In many of the squat variations featured in this book, balance and mobility play a crucial role in execution.

Remember, when it comes to mastering certain exercises, "your strength in them will only be as good as the quality of your movement allows".

No. 11- Stand erect, with legs crossed as shown in the dotted diagram, the hands resting lightly on hips. Sweep front leg well round and to the rear, sinking the body into the position assumed by a lady in the old-style deep curtsey. Return slowly, change legs, and repeat up to five times, increasing once per week to twenty-five repetitions. Extremely trying exercise, especially on the leg muscles, although the abdominals will also benefit considerably.

No. 12- Stand erect, heels together, feet turned out. Extend arms right and left from shoulders and sink down, bending the knees outwards and rising on the toes, until you are almost squatting on your heels. Return to the first position and repeat the bend with arms stretched out in front. Return and again sink with arms stretched above the head. Repeat these three performances daily for the first week and then perform two of each and so on. *One of the best leg exercises in the world.*

No. 13- Take up position as shown in the diagram, the arms to be straight, resting on thumbs and fingers, front leg fairly bent, back leg slightly. The weight to be chiefly supported by the arms. Then, pushing off smartly with rear foot, raising the body thereby, rapidly alternate the position of feet. Spring smartly each time, but not too sharply, to avoid straining the muscles. Practice three times per week on alternate days. Muscles chiefly affected are the extensors and flexors of the thighs and calves, the abdominals, chest, back of the neck, back, and arm muscles.

No. 14- This exercise, popular with Turkish athletes, is of the utmost benefit to the arm muscles, chest, and the whole system generally. Stand about four feet from a wall, slightly overbalanced. Lean against the wall with the full weight supported by the right hand, body slightly turned to the left. Push off smartly so the body sways back and turns to the right, falling towards the wall and being stayed therefrom by the rigid left arm. Push off again smartly with left and meet wall with right. Continue the exercise, as quickly as possible, until tired, gradually increasing the number of repetitions as capacity to withstand the strain develops.

CHAPTER IX

Muscle exercises with weights

ANY male reader who is normally of good physique, who has indulged in any form of athletics, or who has practised the series of exercises dealt with in the last chapter, for a period, say of six months, should, however, devote his principal attention to muscular development. He may secure and maintain a condition of fair physical fitness by means of exercise without weights, such exercises as have been detailed in Chapter VIII; but he cannot hope to become really strong unless he exercises with weights; for it is only by so doing that he can develop muscle of really good quality, and, as already hinted, it is important, both from the Strength and the Health points of view, that every muscular group throughout the body should be of the best quality attainable. Every human being possesses about five hundred separate muscles, but it would be neither necessary nor useful to detail all these here.

For the purposes of development, of culture that is to say, it will be quite sufficient to classify them in groups, such as Neck muscles, Shoulder muscles, Arm muscles, Chest muscles, muscles of the Abdomen, Back, Legs, etc. No one can afford to neglect any of these groups. All, in fact, should be equally developed, those which are naturally weaker to a greater extent than the others, until all are equally strong, when the object in view should be that of equal all-round improvement.

FIRST SERIES FOR THE NECK MUSCLES

Exercise 1- Repeat Exercise No. 1 in the last chapter, i.e., place clasped hands on the back of the neck and press the head downwards on the chest, resisting this pressure by the exercise of the neck muscles. Commence with five repetitions, and increase gradually, say once with every third performance, up to finally twenty repetitions.

Exercise 2.- Reverse the above exercise by pressing the head back against hand resistance and perform as before.

Exercise 3.- Exercise No. 2, dealt with in the last chapter. Stand erect and roll the head in every direction by bending the neck as much as possible. Continue as directed in Exercise 1.

Exercise 4.- Press a bar-bell weighing from 30 lb. to 50 lb. with both hands into the head bridge, as shown in the sketch.

Place a rather hard cushion under the head (a rolled-up coat or the like, if nothing else is available). The body should rest on the heels and crown of the head only. At first, this exercise may not be found easy of accomplishment, in which case the bridge should be perfected before the bar-bell press is attempted. The higher the bridge, the easier will the press be found. Repeat three times to commence with and gradually increase, say once every second week, up to ten repetitions; then add 5 lb. to the bell and commence again with three repetitions and so on. A capital exercise for strengthening the muscles of the neck, nape and spine.

Exercise 5. Get down on hands and knees and hang, by a broad belt, a weight on the back of the head (at first 10 lb. would be sufficient). With this, move the head up, down and to both sides until tired, but not until exhausted.

SECOND SERIES FOR THE NECK, SHOULDER, ARM, AND CHEST MUSCLES

In most systems of Physical Culture I have observed the shoulder muscles to be sadly neglected, and that therefore many otherwise well-developed athletes have narrow and unshapely shoulders. I would therefore wish to see special attention devoted to those exercises in this section, which deal principally with the shoulders. It will have been observed that Exercises 4 and 5 just dealt with exert a beneficial influence on the shoulder muscles (as will many others), but this must on no account be considered as sufficient, and it is because the first three of the present series directly affect the shoulders that I would like to see them regularly practised.

Exercise I- Stand erect as in the sketch, holding a 10 lb. dumb-bell in each hand. Hunch shoulders as high as possible for ten repetitions, increasing by one with every third performance of the exercise up to twenty repetitions; then increase weights by 5 lb. and commence afresh.

Exercise N°. 1

Exercise 2. Then holding arms bent at elbows, roll the shoulders right round and repeat as in the last exercise.

Exercise N°. 2

Exercise 3. Standing erect with a 5 lb. dumb-bell in each hand, hanging at sides, raise same smartly to armpits, each hand alternately, as shown in the sketch. Commence with five repetitions, adding one every week up to ten. Then add 1 lb. to each dumb-bell and commence afresh, and so on.

Exercise N°. 3

Exercise 4. Jerk with both arms from the shoulders a bar-bell of from 30 lb. to 50 lb. in weight, using arm strength only. Jerk both with top and bottom holds, five times each to commence with, adding one repetition per week up to ten. Then add 10 lb. to the bell and commence afresh. Top hold means with the back of the hand pointing upward, as against bottom hold when the back of the hand points downwards.

Exercise N°. 4

Exercise 5— Pull up with both hands, top hold, a bar-bell of from 10 lb. to 15 lb. from the hang to the shoulders as shown in the sketch. The elbow should be held firmly against the sides, the lift to be performed without any movement of the body. Repeat five times, increasing by one every week up to ten times. Then add 5 lb. and commence afresh. (ii) This exercise should also be performed with bottom hold beginning with from 20 lb. to 25 lb., for five repetitions and continuing as with top hold.

Exercise N°. 5

Exercise 6— Press a bar-bell of from 30 lb. to 50 lb. from shoulders to full arm's length above the head. Begin with five repetitions, increasing by one every week up to ten. Then add 5 lb. to the weight and commence afresh. (ii). This exercise to be performed with both top and bottom holds.

Exercise N°. 6

Exercise 7— Jerk a bar-bell of from 25 lb. to 40 lb. from the shoulder, erect above the head, with one arm. The elbow should rest firmly against the hip, thus transferring the whole weight of the bar-bell to the legs, principally to the one leg. Quickly bend the knees, and, at the same time, "throw" the weight upwards, while with the same quick movement you stretch the arm. You will find that the principal impetus of strength will be given by the legs. The movements have to be made very quickly. This particular exercise requires a certain technique. It greatly furthers the preservation of a perfect nimbleness and equilibrium, and develops at the same time the muscles of the legs, forearm, and triceps. The exercise should be performed with both the right and the left arm, at first five times, every second week increasing by one up to ten times, then increase the weight by 5 lb. and start afresh.

Exercise 8,—Parallel bar exercise between two chairs without weight. This exercise can also be performed on the floor, but the body must be kept perfectly rigid. Thus, forearm, shoulder, and abdominal muscles are brought into play. Begin with five repetitions, and increase by one every week, up to twenty repetitions.

Exercise 9.—Lying on the floor, press with both arms with top hold a bar-bell of from 30 Ib. to 50 lb. for five repetitions when exercising, Increase by one every week up to ten times, then add 10 Ib. and start afresh. (ii) This exercise should also be done with bottom hold.

Exercise 10.—Swing a bar-bell of from 15 Ib. to 30 Ib., with straight arms and top hold, from the thigh to full arms' length above the head. Repeat five times, increasing by one by one every week up to ten repetions, then increase weight by 5

THE ANCIENT WAY OF TRAINING

This chapter provides a glimpse into Hackenschmidt's training methods. While some might view it as outdated today, with certain exercises no longer "in circulation", this approach was notably distinct from the norms of his era, which often revolved around performing countless repetitions of single-joint exercises.

The floor press or horizontal push from the ground is performed in its wrestler's bridge variation, supported by the feet and head, offering direct applicability to wrestling positions. Neck-specific exercises are included as essential components, with clear relevance to wrestling performance.

Hackenschmidt's training also emphasizes long-lever exercises for the shoulders and hips, effectively creating significant torque on these joints. Hack himself advises caution with the loads used, which is why he often performed these exercises with hollow globe barbells of lighter weight.

Squats are executed in their traditional style, with heels together and elevated, increasing the relative load on the quadriceps group. This approach underscores the unique and practical aspects of Hackenschmidt's methods, bridging strength training and functional application in combat sports.

Exercise 11,—Lying down full length on the floor, pull over the head with stretched arms to a line with the shoulders a bar-bell of from 10 Ib. to 20 lb. Repeat five times, increasing by one repetition every week up to ten repetitions, and then increase weight by 5 Ib. and start afresh.

Exercise 12.—Lying down as before, with arms out-stretched sideways, lift to arms' length in front Of body a 10 Ib, dumb-bell in each hand. Repeat five times, increasing by one repetition every week 'Up to ten times, then increase weight of dumb-bells Ib. each and start afresh.

Exercise I—Stoop down and pull in to the chest a bar-bell of, say, 30 lb. with top hold. Straighten the shoulders well during the movement. Repeat five times, increasing by one every week up to ten repetitions and then add 5 lb. and start afresh.

Exercise 2.—Stoop down as before and pull in with each hand a 20 Ib. dumb-bell, simultaneously. Repeat five times, increasing as before to ten times, then add 5 Ib. to each bell and start afresh.

Exercise 3.—Press a bar-bell of from 10 Ib. to 20 tb. full reach above the head; then bend forward as shown in sketch. Repeat five times at first, increasing by one every week up to ten repetitions.

Then increase weight by 5 Ib. and start afresh. The hip, abdominal and back muscles are all well benefited by this exercise.

ABS, HIPS, AND LEGS!

An intriguing title that might bring to mind the typical programs offered by gyms aimed at weight loss or targeting popular areas of the body for development. However, when analyzing the functional purpose of the exercises included in this work, it becomes clear that their aim is far from purely aesthetic.

These exercises serve as a bridge between basic movements and barbell exercises, where strength, stability, and mobility are essential. Many of these exercises focus on generating movement primarily at the hip joints while keeping the trunk and lumbar region stable.

Pay close attention to the fact that most of these exercises involve long levers, making proper execution critical. They demand an exceptionally strong core capable of maintaining control and transferring forces between the upper and lower limbs. In all of these movements, it is vital to maintain spinal neutrality while managing or transfering loads.

Exercise 4.—Stoop down and pull up to "hang," as shown in sketch, a bar-bell of from 50 Ib. to 70 Ib. with both hands (top hold), arms and legs to be perfectly straight. See that the hip muscles alone are exercised. Commence with five repetitions, increasing gradually say by one per week up to ten, then increase weight by 10 Ib. and start afresh.

Exercise 5.—Lie down full length on your back "4nd raise both legs, forming a right angle with the body. Repeat five times, adding one repetition weekly up to ten repetitions. Then commence afresh, tying 2.5 kg to each foot.

Exercise 6.—Lie down full length as in last exercise and rise into sitting posture without moving the legs. At first it may be necessary to establish a counter poise by laying a bar-bell over the feet or legs. Repeat five times, increasing as in last up to ten. Then hold a 5 lb. weight against forehead and commence afresh. This weight can afterwards be increased gradually by holding a dumb-bell in each hand close to the head.

A GRIP EXERCISE FOR DEVELOPING THE STRENGTH OF THE HANDS, FOREARMS, ETC.

For Home Use

Get a round stick, a thick broom-handle will do, although it should be from 1 in. to 14 in. thick. Pierce a hole through this and suspend by a cord a 5 Ib. weight. Now stand on two chairs and, holding the bar waist high, roll it round with both hands, winding up the cord. Continue until the weight is wound close up and then unwind to full length. Both wind and unwind with continuous and also with reverse rollings. Continue until tired. The rolling movement to be always steady and gradual.

For Gymnastum Use

For use in gymnasia, schools, etc., a special stand may be constructed, as shown in sketch. In this instance two weights should be used attached to eac Grip Exercise for Home Use Arranged for Gymnasium end of the bar. Five pounds' weight each will be found more than ample to commence with. The roll ings to be performed as for home use, but the bar is, of course, now supported.

FOURTH SERIES OF EXERCISES FOR SPECIALLY DEVELOPING THE LEG MUSCLES

___A note of warning should here be sounded, to the 'effect that, while every one suffering from rupture, or with a tendency to rupture, should be very careful in all exercises, they must be particularly so with leg exercises, These would do well, in fact, to confine their leg movements to those without weights, and in any event to avoid altogether Exercise 5 set forth below.

Nevertheless, if the reader be sound and fit and free from such local weakness as might possibly terminate in rupture, then should he on no account neglect any of the leg exercises; for it must be remembered that while walking, cycling, etc., are good exercises for the leg muscles, yet are they insufficient alone to develop them satisfactorily for the performance of either weight-lifting feats or even of heavy weight-lifting exercises.

Exercise I.—Hold a bar-bell of from 10 Ib. to 20 lb. weight behind the back with arms crossed, heels together, toes pointed outwards. Now make a deep knee bend, rising on your toes, parting your knees, until almost squatting on your heels. Rise again to first position. Repeat five times, adding one repetition per week up to twenty repetitions, after which increase weight by 5 lb. and start afresh. (This exercise is called "Hacke" in Germany.)

Exercise 2—Jumping. Take running and standing high and long jumps, but standing jumps particularly. Jump with and without weights and also practise hop, step and jump; three forward jumps; hop, cross and jump, and all the Lancashire varieties.

Exercise 3.—Skipping exercise, especially with long runs on the toes of one foot, which will be found particularly beneficial to the calf muscles.

Exercise 4.—Hold a bar-bell of from 20 Ib. to 40 Ib. weight with both hands on the shoulders, behind the neck, feet together, and make the deep knee bend without raising the heels. This exercise will specially develop the muscles of the thighs and groin.

Commence with three repetitions, increasing by one every week up to ten repetitions, after which add 5 Ib. and commence afresh.

Exercise 5.—Lying full length on the floor on i: your back, raise your legs well over to an acute angle with your body, bending both at your hips and knees. Pull over your head a bar-bell of from 20 Ib. to 30 Ib. and rest it across the soles of your feet. When this has been well balanced, push your legs Straight, bend them in again, and again push straight. Repeat at first from three to five times according to ability, gradually increasing until ten repetitions tan be made fairly easily, then add 5 Ib. weight and Start afresh.

(N.B.—The weight used and number of repetitions recommended for this exercise can only be approximate. The first essential is to secure and maintain a perfect balance, wherefore a very light bar-bell indeed may be used until a perfect equilibrium).

JOSEF STEINBACH

Origin: Bohemia, Czech Republic.

Period: Classic [1879-1937].

Specialty: Weightlifter - Wrestler

Notable skill: One-handed lifts

Highlight: Winner of 5 European weightlifting championships. First place in the one-handed weightlifting event at the 1906 Olympic Games.

Antagonist: Arthur Saxon (?)

Preferred equipment: Dumbbells

Josef Steinbach was born in Bohemia in 1879. At the age of 15, he moved to Vienna, where he began his career as a weightlifter. He quickly became Austria's top weightlifter, winning the Austrian Athletic Club Association Championship in 1900, the first of many European titles he would claim in the following years.

At the 1906 Olympic Games, he did not win the two-handed lifting event due to unfamiliarity with the rules. However, he succeeded in the dumbbell category (one-handed lifts).

After the Olympics, he became a professional athlete, focusing primarily on wrestling and weightlifting exhibitions.

In 1910, Steinbach issued a public challenge to the famous strongman Arthur Saxon to compete for the title of "World Professional Weightlifting Champion". The announcement was published repeatedly in various physical culture magazines of the time, but Saxon never responded to the provocations.

Steinbach achieved several records, including a one-handed dumbbell lift of 106 kg, which remained unbeaten until 1930.

He passed away in Vienna in 1937. A year later, a group of Austrian and German weightlifters and wrestlers erected a granite monument in his honor.

CHAPTER X
Weights for exercises

WHAT WEIGHT SHOULD ONE EXERCISE WITH?

SOME trainers recommend to their pupils for the training of all muscle groups one and the same (light) weight and believe they are able to obtain the same effect by frequent repetitions. My experience has taught me that this is wrong, for the muscles of men or animals who are distinguished for certain feats of endurance are by no means over-developed. A long-distance runner or long-distance cyclist always has comparatively thin legs, as have a racehorse, stag, and greyhound. Nature does not act without aim and purpose. Hence there is a great difference between feats of endurance and feats of strength. One must consider that, although it is quite possible to enlarge muscles by certain light, prolonged exercise, at the same time the development of the sinews may be neglected, and it is the sinews which transport the action of the muscles to the bone frame. The sinews can only be exercised and strengthened by correspondingly heavy muscle work. Besides, to take a paradoxical example, it is quite impossible to improve strong muscle groups, as, for instance, the hip muscles, with light-weight exercises. A further illustration of the fallacy of attempting to develop the muscles by frequent repetitions with the same light exercises may be found in a comparison with any and every other form of athletics, in which a man would never think of merely repeating his training programme. In order to improve himself either in pace or distance, he must set himself a steady progression of arduous effort.

HOW CAN ONE GAUGE THE MOST SUITABLE WEIGHTS FOR EXERCISE?

This is quite easy. When in an unfatigued condition try an exercise say ten times. If you can accomplish this by using all your strength you have found the proper weight with which to begin your exercises five times in succession.

HOW TO INCREASE THE WEIGHTS AND THE NUMBER OF MOVEMENTS

After having ascertained the correct weight for every exercise, begin each movement, say five times, and increase the number by one every week: thus five one week, six the next, seven the next, etc., until the prescribed maximum is reached. After that begin afresh with a weight that is 5 lb. heavier for one-arm exercises, or 10 lb. for two arms, unless otherwise directed.

WHEN SHOULD ONE BEGIN TRIALS WITH HEAVY WEIGHTS?

This should only be done after one has trained for at least three months in the foregoing manner with light weights, and one should never begin to lift any heavier weight than one can lift without much exertion at least ten times. He who ventures such trials without this previous training exposes himself to strainings or breakings of the sinews or muscles, also to ruptures, and I would particularly caution my readers against any such imprudent experiments.

I strongly recommend at the beginning of training the recording in a book, say every three months, of one's measurements and weights, also of the progress made. The measurements which should be taken are of the following parts: neck (thinnest part); forearm (thinnest part); forearm (thickest part), the arm to be held out and only the fist closed; biceps of arm held straight out; biceps of arm bent; the forearm and biceps measurements to be taken right and left; chest (normal, measured across the nipples); chest (deflated); chest (inflated); wrist (normal); thigh (thickest part); leg (just above the knee); calf. Always take the measurements before any exercises. It is a fact that the first improvement which the muscles undergo is in their quality long before they grow in size. It therefore follows that if the muscles are of fatty or watery nature a diminution in the size of some of them will take place. This is quite a natural consequence, which must be borne in mind, and which must not discourage the pupil in the least. After exercising when undressed, one ought to try by the straining of certain muscle groups to obtain a fine moulding of one's body and a complete mastery over single parts of it. In other words, poses must be practiced to achieve an effect.

WEIGHT, LOAD, AND QUANTITY: THE BIG QUESTION

If we had to summarize Hackenschmidt's proposed training method, it could be encapsulated in his own words:

"The best physical exercise is lifting weights. The method would be to lift the weight from the ground to a position above your head with your arm extended. Do this for a week, then add half a kilo to the bar. Keep lifting this weight until it becomes easy again. Then, continue gradually increasing the load; otherwise, you will end up with an injury instead of a benefit".

These comments are based on the principle of progressive overload, a logical way to train that allows the body's structures to adapt progressively under a constant yet balanced stimulus.

Hack also emphasizes that there is no need to dedicate "grueling hours of training" in the gym. This is advice for the average person who might shy away from strength training, fearing it requires the commitment of a professional lifter. Hack recommends half an hour of daily training for the average person who simply wants to stay in good shape.

This is a sensible suggestion, especially for those who are not accustomed to regular exercise, making strength training approachable and sustainable for the general public.

CHAPTER XI

Exercises for athletes

After having trained three or four months on the system dealt with in the last chapter, a great increase of strength will be soon perceived. If it is intended to further increase it, one should begin to train once or twice per week (provided always one does not possess any tendency to rupture) with heavier weights. I recommend the use for six months only of such weights as one can handle at least five to ten times for one exercise; on such days avoid part of, if not all, ordinary exercises.

There are a great many weight-lifting exercises, which might be mentioned, but I propose here to confine myself to the principal ones for ordinary feats of strength. The bar-bell for this purpose should be 1 1/10 in. thick. Always take a deep breath before each separate lift. Do not wear a tight belt when practising.

I. SNATCH WITH ONE HAND
(right or left)

Rule: The bar-bell is lifted with one hand without stop from floor to full extent above the head.

Execution: Place the bar-bell near both feet over the instep, get hold precisely in the middle, bend down, lay the free hand on the respective knee (left hand on the left knee or right hand on the right knee), take a quick and firm grip, and pull the weight at the same time with a lightning rapidity upwards. The muscles of the hand, forearms, biceps, shoulders, legs, abdomen, and hip should all work together only for a fraction of a second (perhaps hardly one-tenth of a second) to obtain a good result. Many athletes snatch the bar only up to the eyes, after which they get their body underneath like lightning. This indicates great strength of legs and agility.

Several athletes snatch about 180 lb. with one hand. Formerly, when I trained regularly with weights (the reader is, perhaps, aware that in the latter part of my career I gave my attention almost entirely to wrestling), I succeeded at St. Petersburg on April 27th, 1898, in snatching 196 lb. with my right hand from the floor to above my head. This was for many years the world's record.

Approved training rules: A practice for the snatch is the lifting of a bar-bell with one hand about three feet from the floor. Snatch the weight thus up to ten times in succession to get the knack of it, for every athlete has his own personal peculiarities in lifting. By constant practice, each will find out which method of snatch is best suited to himself. When you have managed to lift the weight above the head, make a slight turning movement to learn to hold (fix) and balance it well. In letting down the weight, use both hands.

After one has trained in this manner for four to six months—that is, having always snatched up to ten times and later increased the weight by 1 lb.—one has attained a certain agility and can try the following: Snatch the weight, which you can generally snatch ten times, thrice, increase the weight by 1 lb. to 5 lb., and snatch two or three times; then again increase by a few pounds, and snatch once or twice, and you will ascertain your own record for the time being. Between the trials, do not pause longer than one to two minutes, as otherwise the energy vanishes. It is quite sufficient to try records every three or four weeks, and in the meantime practise thoroughly exercises of endurance, and with light weights try to still improve those muscles which you have found to be somewhat flabby. It is easy to find out in what points one is lacking.

As a matter of course, all one-arm exercises are to be made right and left, so as to obtain the same strength and dexterity in both arms. In carrying out all these exercises it is advisable to walk up and down the room continually between feats.

2. ONE-ARM SWING OF DUMB-BELL

This exercise resembles the foregoing. Use a short dumb-bell.

Rule: The dumb-bell lies between the legs lengthways. The inner side of the front ball to be in line with the toes, and the weight to be raised from the floor to above the head with one movement and one arm. Some athletes stipulate that the free hand should not touch the body anywhere, and to touch the floor with the free hand would disqualify.

Execution: Seize the dumb-bell with your hand against the front ball (not in the middle), bend fairly low, and swing the weight upwards. Some athletes first swing forward to get the momentum; this is permitted. In this performance there are the same advantages as in the snatch. French athletes excel in it. The one-arm swing is often made with ring weights, which are swung between the legs. The Frenchman, Apollon, made a specialty of it, and could swing four weights tied together of 180 lb. total above the head. The German, Belling, was also excellent; he swung 180 lb. three times.

As the swinging of ring weights requires a strong forearm and wrist, it is advisable to fasten a leather strap of two to three inches width round the wrist.

3. ONE-ARM JERK

Rule: The weight, either bar-bell or dumb-bell, is pushed from the shoulder to above the head with one arm, in one jerk. Whilst in England, France, and Italy it is the rule that the weight should be raised to the shoulder with one hand only, it was usual in my country (Russia) and in Germany to employ both hands. The Russian athlete Lurich, who was one of the best specialists in this feat, consequently raised his weight with both hands to the shoulder, and I did the same. If the weight has to be lifted to the shoulder with one arm, one may do this by snatching it or by standing the bar-bell straight up, and getting underneath it. The dumb-bell or bar-bell should, at any rate, rest free on one hand without touching the shoulder.

PRACTICAL HINTS FOR JERKING

Place the elbow of the arm, holding the weight, firmly against the body near the hip, so that the arm is somewhat relieved of the weight. Now bend your knee slightly, and, by sudden rising and pushing upward with shoulder and arm, jerk to full arm's length above your head. Train in the same way as indicated for the one-arm snatch.

ONE-ARM PRESS

Rule: The weight, dumb-bell or bar-bell, is to be raised from the shoulder above the head without swing or jerk of the body or legs, but simply by the strength of the arms; the body may be slightly bent. Here, also, different styles are practiced in different countries in lifting the weight to the shoulders. There is a rule observed in Great Britain and France, but not so much in Germany, for the position of the feet during the performance, namely, the so-called "at attention" position, heels touching in military style, and pressing the weight

UNILATERALITY AND STABILITY

Unilateral work, in addition to introducing a unique challenge, provides an increased demand for stabilization. A barbell positioned on only one side of the body requires extra core engagement, particularly on the side opposite the load.
This type of training offers greater transfer to sports movements, as it can replicate the asymmetrical patterns often seen in athletic activities. The old-time strongmen understood this through empirical experience and the results they achieved.

without the slightest movement of the body. It is evident that under this rule an athlete cannot possibly press more than, say, half his own weight.

A holder of the world's record in the "at attention" position, Michael Maier, of Vienna, was especially adapted for this feat, having very short arms, and being very heavy (243 lbs.). His record was 143 lbs.

There have been obtained a good many noteworthy records in the ordinary one-arm press (endurance and strength feats). At the age of nineteen years, I myself pressed a bar-bell of 269 lbs. with one arm.

Arthur Saxon, the world's record holder, an athlete well known in England, has obtained wonderful results in the one-arm press. He used to bend himself, as it were, under the weight, and has pressed as much as 371 lbs. (bar-bell) with one hand.

I may mention here that some authorities use the expression "screwing" for this kind of performance.

The real difference between "pressing" and "screwing" is, that in pressing the arm propels the weight upwards, whilst in screwing the weight hardly changes its height, as the body changes its position underneath it until the arm is stretched, after which the athlete simply erects himself. The body performance is exactly the same when you stand against the wall and press yourself away from it with one hand. The training for the press is done in the same way as indicated for the one-arm snatch. The so-called "screwing" is, technically, the most difficult kind of weight-lifting, and requires much practice, especially by a young athlete, whose body is still flexible. Its training should, however, be conducted very carefully, and one ought to have a friend assist in lowering the weight, instead of letting it drop. Bent pressing requires a good balance of the body, and great calmness and determination. Press as slowly as possible.

N.O J.M: Screwing is the Bent Press

ONE-HAND LIFTS

One particularly remarkable aspect of this work is the number of one-hand barbell lifts it features. This practice was not unusual for its time. Almost all lifters, even in competitions, performed classic lifts such as the jerk, snatch, bent press, and windmills with one hand.

Today, these unilateral lifts are nearly forgotten, whether due to fear, lack of knowledge, or insufficient stability and motor control. However, they offer the unique ability to lift an inherently unstable tool like a barbell, while also developing control, balance, coordination, and mobility—qualities that are often not as effectively trained with balanced two-hand lifts.

TWO-ARM SNATCH

Rule: The bar-bell is raised in one movement from floor to above the head.

This exercise, like the single-arm snatch, requires lightning rapidity in the simultaneous working of the leg, hip, abdomen, and arm muscles; the whole body is thereby improved simultaneously, both in strength and agility. Here also the correct exercise is the slow but gradual increase from one to five times.

TWO-ARM JERK

Rule: The bar-bell is pushed from the shoulder a jerk to above the head, the legs seconding, and there at least a few seconds.

The bar-bell has to be raised in one movement from the floor to the shoulder. Josef Steinbach, of Vienna, held the world's record with 380 1/4 lbs., raising the bar-bell in more than one movement from the floor to the shoulder. I also jerked, during my training, over 330 lbs. under the same conditions.

For the French style of jerk with both arms (lifting the weight in one movement to the chest), Arvid Anderson made a record with 328 1/2 lbs. Note—Steve Stanko of York, Pa., in December 1939 established a new world's record of 370 pounds in this style.

The increase of the weight to lift during training is to be observed in the same gradual manner. Exercise principally in the usual style (one movement to chest), which is more elegant, and is of greater value. With very heavy weights, however, lift first against the body, and then jerk up to the shoulder in one movement.

Support the weight as much as possible on the top part of the chest;

do not hesitate long however, but push vigorously upwards, trying to straighten the arms as quickly as possible, and to get underneath the bar-bell. These giant performances are only possible by the exercise of consummate technique, combined with strength. The best position of the legs is soon found out by the performer himself. Some take a step by putting one leg forward, some backward; some spread their legs much, others less. I have witnessed good results in all these positions; all depends on the individual manner.

TWO-ARM PRESS

Rule: The weight is to be raised from the shoulders above the head by the strength of the arms only, without the help of the body or legs, and fixed for a few seconds.

Here, again, the modus operandi is different in various countries. In Germany and Austria, particularly, there are a great many athletes who are very skilled in the two-arm press. This performance is technically the simplest and easiest kind of weight-lifting, as only the muscles of the shoulders and triceps are brought into play.

Training should be done in the same way as for single-arm press or

116

push. On the Continent, these eight styles of weight-lifting, viz., one-arm right and left snatch, jerk and press, both-arm jerk and press, are called the "Achtkampf," or the eight-lift competition, and they form, as it were, the classical test of strength.

There have, however, been established records in various other forms of weight-lifting, of which I will only mention the more important ones.

LIFTING IN THE BRIDGE

I have already recommended this exercise as excellent for the development of the spine, neck, and nape muscles, under the heading of neck muscle exercises.

I will, therefore, only mention the world's record obtained by myself on August 2, 1898, in Vienna, of 311 lb.

FREE LIFT TO CHEST IN ONE MOVEMENT

This exercise is practised principally in England, France and Italy, where it is regarded as being the only correct style for all double-arm lifts. It forms a preliminary exercise for the double-arm snatch.

Records: Pierre Bonnes (Paris), 330 lb.; Eliseyeff (Russia), 330 lb. I have also lifted in this style 308 lb.

THE HORIZONTAL EQUIPOISE OF WEIGHTS
(Balancing weights with arms outstretched sideways.)

In France this performance ranks among the classical feats of strength for athletes, and there exist definite rules for its execution:

1. The arm holding the weight to form exactly a right angle with the body, rather lower than higher.
2. The arm and wrist must be fully stretched.
3. The body must be perfectly straight, and lean in no direction.

There are two ways of performing this feat, namely:

1. The balancing of the weight on the hand, which is the less difficult.

In this case the weight is of the oblong shape used for weighing purposes, and is slightly hollowed out at the bottom, so that there is an edge. It is held so that the palm of the hand presses against this edge, while the one part of the weight rests on the wrist, and the finger-tips touch the other end.

One may lift the weight with both hands to the shoulder, and press it up and then let it down into the balance, or, which is considered better style, one may raise it directly sideways into the balance. It has to be fixed for a few seconds in the proper balance before being released. The weights, according to their size and heaviness, have a width from 8 to 12 in. at the bottom.

For the two-arm balance, the weights are placed with a side on the hand, so that the bottom and top of the weights are seen. In balancing, the body must not be bent backwards (which would make it easier, but which counts so many points less).

The records of this difficult performance are held by the French professional athlete Victorius, who has balanced 82½ lb. on the hand and 66 lb. by the ring.

In a less strictly correct style, I balanced on February 15, 1902, with both arms, dumb-bells of 90 lb. in the right hand and 89 lb. in the left hand simultaneously, and have even held out 110 lb. right and 100 lb. left, simultaneously, although my performance could not be claimed as a record, seeing that it did not conform exactly to the regulations.

2. Balancing with ring weights is simpler in the hold, but more difficult to execute, as the palm is held downwards. The ring can, therefore, only be held

against the thumb (which is more or less painful) or against the finger-ends. The weight is generally raised with slightly bent arms to the shoulders, and then held out sideways. Some prominent athletes lift it straight from the floor into the balance, and, as this is especially difficult, it counts higher.

IMPRESSIVE RECORDS?

Some of the numbers achieved in the lifts of this era might seem modest, even insignificant, by today's standards. However, as with everything analyzed in this book, it's crucial to understand these feats within the context in which they occurred:

- These were the first times such exercises were performed, with little to no historical precedent. All the advice, recommendations, and accumulated experiences we now have after 150 years of training simply didn't exist back then. For instance, the bench press only began to appear at the end of the 1800s, initially performed lying on the floor. This meant it was a completely new movement, with no established techniques or guidelines to follow—making it more limited.

- Records are always built on previous records. Each new record benefits from the knowledge, experiences, and methods developed by the previous generation. For example, to lift more than 100 kilograms, subsequent lifters had not only the information from their predecessors but also more time to refine techniques and learn from both their successes and failures.

Hackenschmidt was perhaps the first to lift over 165 kilograms in the floor press (the precursor to the modern bench press), a record he held for years until it was surpassed with the invention of the bench and rack. His deadlift records exceeded 260 kilograms—a mark later raised to 320 kilograms by Hermann Goerner. This progression laid the foundation for today's records, which now surpass 500 kilograms.

Execution methods also presented unique challenges. The "bench press" was performed on the floor, with lifters positioning themselves beneath the weight and sometimes using hip thrusts to move the bar—without the assistance of a rack.

Squats were executed with heels together and elevated off the ground, resulting in a shallow range of motion. Grossenhain managed to lift 200 kilograms using this technique in 1899. Over time, empirical discoveries revealed that increasing foot width, planting the full foot on the ground for stability, and engaging the glutes more by flexing the hips allowed lifters to achieve more than double the weights managed by the old-time strongmen.

It's also worth noting that lifters of this era had no access to modern ergogenic aids, further highlighting the raw nature of their accomplishments.

The following are a few further records in weight-lifting and athletic performances:

Both arm press with two weights.
Wilhelm Tiirck, Vienna, on August 29, 1899: 140 lb. dumb-bell in the right hand, 139½ lb. dumb-bell in the left hand, together 279½ lb., lifted to shoulder and correctly pressed.
The same on August 29, 1899, at Vienna: 300 lb. bar-bell lifted to the shoulders with both arms and pressed.

Schneider, Cologne (Germany), 1897: 100 lb. dumb-bell in each hand, twelve times.

Wilhelm Tiirck, Vienna, on July 30, 1901: two so-called "Boli" dumb-bells, 286 lb., correct from the shoulder to above the head.
(The lift to the shoulders was done in each case in several movements.)

Press from sitting posture (both arms).
Wilhelm Tiirck, on September 25, 1900: (sitting on a chair) bar-bell of 220 lb. four times, bar-bell of 237 lb. twice, bar-bell of 253 lb. once.

Lying on the floor and pulling bar-bell over the head and press.
George Hackenschmidt (record), August 2, 1898, in Vienna, 333 lb.

Pushing bar-bell while lying on the floor.
George Hackenschmidt (record), 360 lb. once (the whole body remaining on the floor).

Deep knee bending without weights.
Max Danthage, Vienna (amateur), on June 4, 1899, 6,000 times correctly within three hours.

Deep knee bending with weight on the shoulder (bar-bell):
H. Sell, Grossenhain (Saxony), on January 21, 1899, 440 lb. seven times.
H. P. Hensan, Copenhagen, on March 19, 1899, 277 lb. sixty-five times.

Deep-knee bending, holding a bar-bell above the head with both hands.
Gustav Wain, at Reval (Russia), on January 13, 1898, 189 lb. four times.

Deep knee bend, holding a weight in each hand above the head.
G. Lurich, at Leipzig, on September 24, 1900, 110 lb. ring weight in each hand, once.

Sitting in Turkish style, and getting up with bar-bell.
George Hackenschmidt, performed at Siebert's Athletic Training School at Alsleben, Germany, in January 1902: holding bar-bell of 187 lb. and getting up, once; holding bar-bell of 110 lb. and getting up, five times.

Press with the feet.
(The athlete lies on his back and raises the bar-bell on the soles of the feet.)
A German amateur, Rudolf Klar, of Leipzig, has pressed in this manner 253 lb. twenty times.

Arthur Saxon could support a tremendous weight on his feet in this position, probably as much as 2,500 lb.

Holding a weight (bar- or dumb-bell) with one hand erect above the head, from standing posture to lying down and getting up again.
This is an exercise which requires great strength and skill. The Swiss professional athlete, Emile Dériaz, at Paris, December, 1903, performed it with a dumb-bell of 189 lb., which he lifted first in one movement to the shoulders and pressed.

Lifting a bar-bell of 14 in. diameter with one hand from the floor.
This performance indicates large hands and a tremendous gripping power. A Leipzig amateur thus lifted 488 lb.; it is true, only about 3½ in. from the ground.

But there are athletes in Germany and Austria who can lift 420 to 440 lb. with one arm from bend to erect position of the body (hang).

Lift of bar-bell with both hands (top hold) from the floor, about six inches.
This requires great strength of arms and legs, especially strength of hips. When out of training, I lifted in Munich about 550 lb.; now a German is said to have lifted 583 lb.

John Terry, York Bar Bell Club lifter; 132-pound champion of the United States, lifted 600 pounds with reverse grip until his back was straight.
This is the present world's record.

CHAPTER XII
Time tables for training

IN consequence of repeated inquiries, I would here suggest a general classi-fication of daily training, for leisured persons, invalids, etc., which may be followed or altered as individual circumstances require:

7 a.m. —Rise, short cold rub or bath (this can be changed to tepid in winter if desired), drying preferably by exercise afterwards, but failing this by vigorous application of a rough towel. In any event, fifteen to twenty minutes' light exercises to follow the bath.

8 a.m.—Breakfast, followed by long walk till 11 a.m.

11 till 12 noon—Vigorous exercises of any kind.

1:30 p.m.—Luncheon, and if needed, one hour's sleep to follow.

5 to 6 p.m.—Vigorous exercise for all muscles.

7:30 p.m.—Dinner, and after rest or recreation out of doors as far as possible.

11 p.m.—Bed-time.

(Sundays, no exercises, but a good brisk walk or walks).

I expect that the majority of my readers, after perusing the above tables, will exclaim: "Yes, this is all very nice, and no doubt useful, but I have neither the time nor the money to live in this style."

To them, I would reply that I wished in the first instance to lay down a proper mode for training for those Physical Culture pupils whose position in life allows of their giving to it all their time for a period of a few months. If anyone should wish to excel and to become a professional athlete, he would in any case have to devote his whole time to physical culture.

SUMMER TIME

Rise an hour before they have to leave for work, have a short cold rub or bath, then light-weight exercises as described according to muscles which specially need development, till the body dries, or if a towel be used, this should be rough and vigorously applied.

Then ordinary breakfast, and walk, instead of taking a bus or trains, part of the way to work. In the train sit, if possible, near the open window.

7 p.m.—Good meal and rest.

Afterwards vigorous exercises.

10:30 p.m.—Bed-time. Keep bedroom windows wide open in summer.

In all cases not less than eight hours' sleep.

WINTER TIME

Rise half an hour later than in summer, for bath, use tepid water, don't spare the towel unless the preferable mode of drying the body by exercise be adopted. Light exercises afterwards. Breakfast, then the same walk and manner of getting to business. Needless to say, in winter in particular, avoid draughts when you feel hot, but, otherwise, do not think that every breath of fresh air is a draught. In the evening, follow the same regime. Keep your bedroom well ventilated (during day and night), have sufficient bed-clothes, but no fires in the bedroom. Don't expose your feet to harm by the use of a warming pan or hot-water bottle.

THE WAY OF LIFE

The training methods suggested by Hackenschmidt extend far beyond weightlifting. He also encourages running (fast and explosively), jumping, and training by striking bags with all parts of the body. This reflects a holistic approach to development—a man or woman capable of moving at any speed, in all planes, and under any conditions. While this model aligns perfectly with the demands of a sport like wrestling, it also meets the needs of a "human" in daily life as well as in the pursuit of personal growth and longevity.

All these exercises are enhanced by frequent cold showers, a practice that aligns with methods regaining popularity in our modern era. Hackenschmidt also emphasizes that there is no "crime" in occasionally enjoying a glass of wine or a cigarette, as long as it is done in a controlled manner, both physically and mentally.

In this way, strength, agility, cardiovascular health, and regeneration, combined with the nourishment of the spirit and controlled indulgences, form a unified approach to living—a comprehensive way of life.

REMEMBER

- That excessive and rapid exercising is harmful. Overwork, like laziness, is harmful.

- To go ahead gently. Increase your weights and exercises gradually and slowly.

- That perseverance only brings permanent strength.

- To give their attention to all parts constituting their corporate frames, for real strength is all-round strength.

- Avoid tight clothing when indoors, even dispensing with collar and coat, if practicable.

- When exercising, wear little or no clothes, or wear light, short, and wide knickers, and so-called gymnasium shoes.

- Don't wear a tight belt.

- Put sweater on during intervals, after having rubbed the perspiration off.

- Avoid late suppers.

- For weights, I recommend disc bells: these can be charged accurately, and do not entail the expens of many various dumb- or bar-bells of the heavier calibre

- Perform your weight-lifting in the open, if possible, otherwise on the ground floor or in a good cellar, but never on top floors.

- If indoors, perform on thick planks or a thick mat.

The tables for exercises mentioned should be compiled by each individual himself, according to his own judgment, based on his own observations. He must adapt them to his age and particular physical and mental constitution, My indications of weights and repetitions of the movements for each exercise will help.

And above all, remember always to walk up and down during any rest between or during exercise, Milton* says: "Don't accuse nature, she has fulfilled her task; you must fulfil yours."

*Note by J.M.: Refers to John Milton, an English poet and essayist, best known for his epic poem "Paradise Lost".

CHAPTER XIII

Dr. von Krajewski, the father of athletics
and his system of life

I HAVE previously stated that doctors, surgeons, and other medical authorities who decry rational, systematic physical exercise—and particularly, exercise
with heavy weights—do so simply because they have never properly studied the
subjects in question.

They may have taken a prejudice, or rather evolved a prejudice, against the
methods which I have ventured to style "The way to live," and having taken up
this attitude, have either refused to make a personal test of them, or have not
been favoured with opportunities for so doing.

For the sake, therefore, of any reader who may have these prejudices, or
who may wish to combat them, I now propose to give a short sketch of a very
eminent medical man, who, having his attention drawn to physical culture at the
age of forty-one, felt himself impelled to make a thorough and complete study
of the subject; and also of the results of his investigation.

I shall frequently have occasion to refer to this doctor in the course of the
story of my life, reference to which will show how well I was situated to form
an exact observation of his daily life.

Indeed, I may say that I owe practically all that I have and am to him. He it
was who taught me how to live and how to train, and he it was who launched
me on my career. Would that I possessed the eloquence to express my life-long
gratitude and my veneration for his memory.

Nor would I indeed claim to be his chief and only debtor. In a sense, perhaps, I owe more to him than anyone else, but athletes the world over are, one
and all, directly or indirectly in his debt. Well was he styled the "Father" of
athletics; for it was on the system which he first organized that every athlete of
any prominence during the last twenty-five or thirty years developed his powers.

On that system and on no other, have Sandow, Saxon, Padoubny, Pierre Bonnes, Zbysco, Siegfried, Aberg, Lurich, Koch, Steinbach and hosts of others developed their powers. The doctor's system may have been varied slightly in individual cases, but the general idea, the general system and routine, nay, almost the entire programme, has in each separate instance followed closely that which Dr. von Krajewski mapped out for himself.

And he, remember, was a convert. He, one of the leading physicians in St. Petersburg, was attracted to the subject of physical exercise as a method of securing and preserving health, strength, activity, and vigour (both mental and physical). The subject appeared interesting to him, he investigated it, approved—and immediately set to work to organize and systematize it.

First and foremost he laid it down that every man should sleep regularly for eight hours out of every twenty-four.

To this end, he would regularly, every night, on retiring to rest, write on a card the hour at which he did so; which card he would throw out into the passage by his bedroom door. When his servant picked this up in the morning he knew at what hour the Doctor was to be called; viz., eight hours after the hour on the card, neither a moment sooner nor later. Say that he had retired at four a.m. Then he would be called at noon, and so forth. Usually, however, he slept from 1 a.m. till 9 a.m., at which hour he would have coffee and rolls, and attend to his correspondence until 10 a.m.

He then adjourned to his gymnasium, a large apartment, fitted with a bath, and having two very large windows, so that as much sunlight as possible might enter. The windows, however, were never opened during the period of exercise, in order that the temperature might be as even as possible.

He would first take a short bath, in water as cold as could be obtained, and in St. Petersburg the water can be cold on occasion. Leaving the bath he never used a towel, but commenced exercise straight away, and continued this for half an hour, at the end of which he would be perfectly warm and dry.

The routine followed was on the lines indicated in chapters IX and XI (for he always exercised with weights). Naturally, it would not have been possible to perform every exercise described in these chapters every day, but a sufficient programme was followed to bring every muscle into play, and this was so varied as to neglect none of the movements.

Between the various exercises he never sat down to rest, but walked steadily up and down the room, with perhaps a wrap thrown over his shoulders (but this rarely).

The exercise finished, he dressed and set forth on his morning round. Having visited his patients he returned home, usually about 2 p.m., for luncheon. After this he slept for one hour, and then commenced receiving patients up till 6 p.m., or thereabouts, which with other duties, occupied him till dinner time (from seven till eight), when he resumed his attendance on indoor patients, who continued to call till as late as midnight, or even later.

This lastmay seem strange to British readers, but I may mention that Russian hours are much later than English ones, and that Dr. Krajewski had an enormous practice, as many as 250 patients frequently calling on him in one day.

I may add that he was a most charitable man, attending numberless patients of the poorer classes without any fee or recompense. These were freely invited to call on him, and used to flock in in large numbers after 8 p.m., as they left their work; his waiting-rooms being usually crowded at that hour.

He had, of course, a large practice among the wealthy classes, which occupied the earlier part of the day.

Needless to say, such an incessant round of hard mental work and anxiety was very wearing, and would have been thought to tax the strength of even the hardiest constitution. Yet the Doctor was always well, active and vigorous in mind and body, and ascribed his perpetual fitness solely to his daily physical exercise.

THE GOOD DOCTOR

There is little to add to Hack's personal description of this pivotal figure in the world of physical culture. Founder of prestigious athletic clubs and personal physician to the Tsar of Russia, Dr. Krajewski is arguably one of the key figures, alongside Professor Atilla and Edmond Desbonnet, responsible for the emergence and development of the greatest strongmen and modern physical culture. Krajewski was a leading advocate and patron of wrestlers and strongmen of his era. Among his most notable students were George Hackenschmidt, Georg Lurich, and Ivan Poddubny, all renowned wrestlers and strongmen who followed his methods and guidance.

As I have said, he did not commence the practice of this until he was forty-one years of age, and yet at sixty-three he always claimed, and was acknowledged, to look younger, and to be far more active and vigorous than he was at forty.

So satisfied was he of the great benefits accruing from systematic physical exercise, that he spared no pains to extend its practice. His enthusiasm and interest were unbounded, while the pains which he would take to enrol adherents and to cultivate promising athletes were almost beyond belief. Some idea of these last may be gathered from a perusal of the "Story of My Life," which I have been persuaded would prove of sufficient interest to publish at length, and with which I therefore propose to conclude this book.

THE STORY OF MY LIFE

I will, possibly, interest my readers to learn some details of my life and of the powers of my physical development.

I was born on July 20, 1878 (Old Style), or August 2, according to English methods of reckoning, at Dorpat, in Russia, my father being the proprietor of some dye-works there. I have a brother and a sister younger than myself.

Both my father and my mother were of average stature, neither of them displaying any unusual physical characteristics, but both my brother and sister possess more than average strength. My grandfather, the father of my mother— who, by the way, I never knew, as he died when I was only three years old—was always described to me as a big and powerful man. He had migrated to Russia from Sweden some sixty years before. My mother always told me that I was very like my grandfather, except that he was rather taller, being six feet in height.

So far as I can remember, I was, from my earliest years, devoted to all bodily exercises, and by the time I was eight or nine years old.

I used to order about a small army of boys of my own age—being admittedly the strongest of them all.

I was sent to the Dorpat Grammar School (Realschule), and soon showed a preference for the hours spent in the gymnasium.

At a gymnastic competition in the year 1891, when I was fourteen years old, I won a prize as the best gymnast of my own age, a fact which my instructor Herr Drewes, a German, communicated to the Press in Germany. At that date, I was 4 ft. 7¾ in. in height and weighed 8 st. 10 lb., being of a rather thick-set build. I was one of the best at club and dumb-bell exercises and could jump over 16 ft. in length and 4 ft. 7¾ in. in height. I could raise and lower a dumb-bell weighing 1 pood (36 lb.) sixteen times with the right hand and twenty-one times with the left, and I once ran 180 metres (about 197 yards) in 26 seconds.

My liking for bodily exercises I inherited from my grandfather. On leaving school in 1895, I entered some large engineering works in Reval as an apprentice, with a view to becoming a practical and technical engineer.

But—Man proposes, God disposes!

At this time I became a member of the Reval Athletic and Cycling Club, and threw myself heart and soul into cycling, at which I won several prizes. When autumn and bad weather came round, I gave more attention to exercises with heavy weights and dumb-bells and my ambition soon led me to excel all my fellow members in these exercises.

The chief pastimes favoured in our club were the lifting of heavy weights and wrestling. For the latter I had at first but little liking and was often beaten.

About this time I grew pretty quickly, my measurements in 1896, at the age of eighteen, being as follows:

Height . . 5 ft. 7¾ in.
Chest . . 41¾ in. normal and 44 in. expanded.
Biceps . . 14 in. straight and 15½ in. flexed.
Forearm . 12¾ in.

We had a very judicious trainer in our club, a certain Gospodin (Mr.) Andruschkewitsch, a government official, who gave us young fellows many excellent hints on the care and training of the body. At a Club festival held about this time (autumn of 1896) I performed the following weight-lifting feats:

With the right hand from the shoulder I pressed . . 145 lb. 12 times
Ditto, ditto . . 155 lb. 10 times
Ditto, ditto . . 198 lb. 3 times
Ditto, ditto . . 214 lb. 1 time

And with one hand lifting slowly from the ground to the shoulder (by the strength of the biceps) I raised a weight of 125 lb. with the right, and of 119 lb. with the left.

In September 1896, I made the acquaintance of the professional athlete and wrestler, Lurich. He was only a few years older than myself, had been a professional for a year, and was touring in the Eastern Provinces with a small company.

Lurich challenged all comers to wrestle with him and various members of our club came forward but were all, without exception, defeated by him. Up to this time, I had shown but little taste for wrestling and had wrestled very seldom, being more partial to work with heavy weights. Still, I wrestled several times with Lurich, who, even then, was a fairly good wrestler, though, as I speedily recognized, scarcely my equal in strength. As can readily be understood, Lurich had no great difficulty in throwing an inexperienced man, such as I was, though on the one occasion on which I wrestled with him in public—in the Standpfort Etablissement in Reval—he could not throw me the first time, and in the second bout I was able to resist him for seventeen minutes.

GEORG LURICH

Russian Empire (Present-day Estonia) [1876-1920]

Georg Lurich was a Greco-Roman wrestler who rose to fame at the beginning of the 20th century. He was a companion and inspiration to many wrestlers, including his fellow Estonians George Hackenschmidt and Aleksander Aberg.
Lurich became involved in sports during his childhood, primarily as a way to escape bullying from his Baltic peers who discriminated against him. After graduating in 1894, he moved to St. Petersburg, where he trained in weightlifting and Greco-Roman wrestling under the guidance of Dr. Krajewski. Lurich was the first Estonian to achieve world records in weightlifting.

His success in wrestling and weightlift-ing, combined with his charisma and the support of the press, made him a highly popular figure in his country, helping to popularize physical culture there.

In 1896, he met a young George Hacken-schmidt, whom he trained for a period of time.
In 1913, alongside his companion Alek-sander Aberg, Lurich traveled to the United States to face Frank Gotch but was unable to defeat him. Upon returning to Europe, he found himself trapped in Russia during the closing stages of World War I.

Lurich died prematurely in a typhoid fever epidemic in 1920 at the age of 43.

G. LURICH.   REVAL (RUSSIE)

I mention this easily intelligible defeat, incurred when I had had little or no experience in wrestling, because, later on, Lurich used to boast that he had frequently beaten me.

This gentleman has, since then, for many years kept carefully out of my way, but this defeat annoyed me and after it, I wrestled more frequently and, in the course of the winter, defeated nearly all the members of our club.

In February 1897, a German wrestler, Fritz Konietzko, came to Reval. It was said that at Magdeburg, he had beaten the famous Tom Cannon, then in his prime, who, in his day, had often wrestled with Abs, a wrestler who enjoyed a big reputation in Germany, and had thus achieved some celebrity in the Greco-Roman style. Konietzko was a rather smaller man than myself, being 5 ft. 6¼ in. in height and barely turning the scale at 165 lb. Taking him all around, his was not a very imposing figure. Yet he was very quick and possessed a strength of hand which to me seemed almost uncanny. These qualities enabled him to defeat all his opponents, especially as he was always undermatched. I was the only member of the amateur contingent to withstand the German. We wrestled for ten minutes without a fall. Not long after this, Ladislaus Pytlasinski, the Polish wrestler, then at the zenith of his fame, came to Reval and, of course, defeated Konietzko.

Pytlasinski defeated me easily, and we all learned a great deal from this great expert of the wrestling arena. In the following year, he was the first wrestler to defeat the famous Turk, Kara Ahmed, in Paris. I remember, too, a very powerful village schoolmaster in the neighborhood of Reval who was one of the chief opponents of this professional wrestler. He (the schoolmaster) had only a few holds, with which he defeated his opponents. On one occasion, he got me down in seven minutes.

As I have said already, these defeats proved very instructive to me, and I gradually, if slowly, began to perfect myself in wrestling.

I improved rapidly in lifting power and also in general physical development, and by July 1897, I was able to press a bar weighing 243 lb. with both hands from my shoulders to the full stretch of my arms. Even at this date, I established a world's record—which was, of course, very soon broken but afterward improved on and since maintained by myself. With my hands crossed behind my back and my knees bent, I lifted a ball weighing 171 lb. This feat proved that I was fairly strong in the legs. Taking two balls weighing 94¼ lb. each in either hand, I swung them with a single motion from the ground to the full stretch of the arms.

Our instructor, Gospodin Andruschkewitsch, took my measurements in December 1897, with the following results:
- Height: 5 ft. 8¼ in.
- Neck: 18¼ in.
- Biceps: 15½ in. straight and 17½ flexed.
- Forearm: 13 in.
- Wrist: 7¼ in.
- Chest: 44½ in. normal and 46 in. expanded.
- Thigh: 23¼ in.
- Calf: 15¼ in.
- Weight: 12 st. 8 lb.

In December 1897, I performed the following feats:
- Jerked up a bar of 216 lb. twelve times with both hands.
- Jerked up a bar of 187 lb. seven times with one hand.
- Pressed up a bar of 216 lb. with one hand.

About this time, I was thrown in contact with a remarkable man, who exercised a notable influence on my future life.

A slight injury sustained in the exercise of my calling as an engineer—for I was still an amateur—made it necessary for me to seek the help of a doctor. This doctor, an amiable old gentleman, happened to have staying with him a distinguished colleague, Dr. von Krajewski, a physician in ordinary to His Majesty the Czar. Dr. von Krajewski was the founder of the St. Petersburg Athletic and Cycling Club, of which H.R.H. the Grand Duke Vladimir Alexandrovitch was President, and which included many aristocratic and wealthy people among its members. Dr. Krajewski, in spite of his fifty-six years, was still a very active and energetic man, and particularly keen on feats of strength and weightlifting.

ALEXANDER ZASS (The Iron Samson)

Vilnius, Russia (Lithuania) [1888-1962]

A pioneer in the implementation of isometric training for strength development, Zass became famous for bending iron bars, breaking chains, and performing feats of support and carrying.

During World War I, Zass served as a soldier in the Russian Army cavalry, fighting against the Austrian Empire. He was captured as a prisoner of war four times but managed to escape on each occasion. While imprisoned, Zass pushed and pulled against the bars and shackles of his cell to maintain his strength. This experience led to the development of his strength training method using isometric exercises and "maximum tensions".

Zass also published his training system and method through correspondence courses. His pamphlet, Samson's System & Methods, is considered the Holy Grail of isometric exercises and a coveted collector's item.

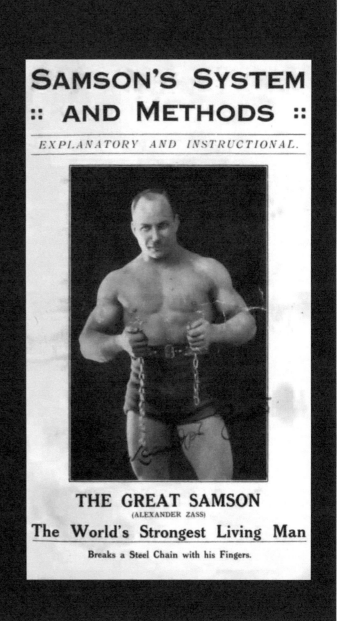

SAMSON'S SYSTEM :: AND METHODS ::

EXPLANATORY AND INSTRUCTIONAL.

THE GREAT SAMSON
(ALEXANDER ZASS)
The World's Strongest Living Man
Breaks a Steel Chain with his Fingers.

He had first taken up this pastime at the mature age of forty-one, and by systematic training, had attained to a fairly high degree of physical strength. The doctor had, of course, visited our club and recognized me at once.

When I had completely undressed in order to facilitate a careful examination of my injury, he, in conjunction with my own doctor, examined my body and found that, with the exception of a slight injury (a contusion of the arm), I was perfectly sound. He invited me to come and stay with him in St. Petersburg, as he wished to have me trained as a professional athlete and wrestler.

I learned that Dr. von Krajewski had also had Lurich in training with him for some time, and he was good enough to say that I possessed possibilities of becoming the strongest man in the world.

Yielding to the persuasion of all my club friends, who congratulated me warmly on Dr. von Krajewski's offer, but against the wishes of my parents, I set out for St. Petersburg early in 1898.

THAT FASCINATION WITH NUMBERS!

The amount of weight lifted seems to be an obsessive constant in old strength training books. This meticulous focus on comparing oneself to others, often over differences of just a few grams, seems to have survived almost unhealthily to the present day. In every old book or manual, we find an extraordinarily DETAILED description of the weight lifted, immediately followed by comparisons to what other lifters could or couldn't achieve.

When someone's lift exceeded others, it was highlighted, cited, and repeatedly celebrated as a definitive victory. However, when a lift fell short, the difficulty of the exercise, the shape of the weight, or the technique used (if it was harder, irregularly shaped, or even if the surface was slippery or unsuitable) was quickly used as justification. These explanations simply sought to emphasize who was the best performer.

Remember, during this era, proving who was stronger was almost a matter of survival. Strongmen performed in theaters and shows where audience numbers depended largely on the amount of weight they could lift.

We also find that the lack of precise measuring tools of the time led to constant comparisons based on body part measurements and sizes, used as a benchmark among competitors or performers.

Dr. von Krajewski was a bachelor and lived in a large house in the Michael Platz, St. Petersburg. He had an excellent practice in the highest circles of society and was reputed to be a millionaire. I was most hospitably received in the house of this patron of athletics. The doctor treated me like a son and gave me the best training his experience could suggest. One room in his house was hung with portraits of all the best-known strongmen and wrestlers, and he delighted in inviting them to his house, where all foreign athletes found a hospitable welcome every month.

Dr. von Krajewski was the organizer of a private club of men of fashion who came to him weekly and worked hard with weights and dumb-bells, and practiced wrestling. His gymnasium contained a great number and variety of weights, dumb-bells, and other apparatus for training purposes. It was, in short, a fully equipped school of physical culture.

All the professional strongmen and wrestlers who appeared at the St. Petersburg theatres visited Dr. von Krajewski and gave exhibitions of their art. While so doing, they were all carefully examined, measured, and weighed. Dr. von Krajewski had thus acquired great experience and knowledge of feats of strength and methods of training.

The example set by these athletes had a most stimulating influence on us all. Everyone seemed determined to do their very best. Having nothing to occupy me but alternate exercise and rest, I made rapid progress in strength. The doctor advised me to avoid alcoholic drinks and tobacco, for neither of which I had ever felt any great inclination, and in neither of which I had ever indulged.

I drank little else but milk (3 liters, or more than 11 pints daily) and ate practically what I pleased, my appetite being excellent, as always. I bathed daily with the doctor in his bath-room, a very spacious apartment built close to the gymnasium. After the bath, we practiced weightlifting until we got dry, neither of us using a towel.

In January 1898, I pushed up a bar weighing 275 lb. to the full height of my arms and with the right hand pushed up 243 lb. Lying on the ground, I lifted and pushed up a weight of 304 lb. with two hands, soon followed by one of 335 lb. With bent knees, I raised a weight of 180¾ lb., which remained a world record for many years until I beat it with 187 lb. in 1902.

In February, I accompanied Dr. von Krajewski to Moscow, where Baron Kister, another great patron of athletics, had organized a weightlifting competition for amateurs. I was fairly successful here, managing to raise a weight of 255¾ lb. with one hand. For this feat, I was awarded a gold medal by my club, the St. Petersburg Athletic and Cycling Club, of which I had become a member. The training at Dr. von Krajewski's was very comprehensive, and I rapidly gained strength in all parts of the body. I also trained steadily in wrestling, the frequent visits of professional wrestlers to the doctor's house providing excellent opportunities.

Around this time, Count Ribeaupierre, Master of the Horse to His Majesty the Czar, became President of the St. Petersburg Athletic and Cycling Club. This gentleman took a keen interest in me and has continued to show goodwill toward me ever since. He frequently supported and helped me, and I feel I owe him a debt of gratitude.

In April 1898, my club organized a weightlifting competition for the championship of Russia, in which I won first prize, achieving the following feats:

- With both hands, I lifted 114 kilograms (251 lb.) to the full height of my arms with a jerk, only 1 kilogram less than the world record held by the Frenchman, Bonnes (115 kilograms).
  - I snatched up 256 lb. with both hands.
  - With my right hand, I jerked 231 lb.
  - With my left hand, I jerked 205 lb.
  - With my right hand, I pressed 269 lb.

Toward the end of April, the famous French wrestler Paul Pons came to St. Petersburg. I defeated this practiced wrestler at the end of forty-five minutes. I also threw Jankowsky in eleven minutes. It is possible that Pons may not have been in his best form on this occasion, as he himself maintained, for some time afterward, I had a much tougher struggle with him.

I was in tip-top condition and was continuing to train steadily when Dr. von Krajewski put down my name to contest the championship of the world and the championship of Europe, at the end of July and beginning of August, which were to be wrestled for in connection with the Sports Exhibition in Vienna.

In order to accustom myself to appearing before large audiences, I performed for some weeks previously in a circus at Riga, as an athlete and wrestler, under an assumed name. Dr. von Krajewski, who had an eye for everything, did not omit to take into account the embarrassment which a young performer is certain to feel when he first faces a large audience. I earned a good deal of applause and threw all opponents in wrestling. But to be quite candid, even at that time I still possessed but little of the technique of wrestling. I was, however, very strong and took all my opponents unawares in a few minutes. Even my former conqueror, Kalde, the teacher already mentioned, was obliged to admit this, as I threw the good man repeatedly after very short struggles, at which he was not a little surprised. Before we set out for Vienna, Dr. von Krajewski took careful measurements of me, with the following results:—

St. Petersburg

- Height: 5 ft. 9½ in.
- Weight: 14 st.
- Waist: 32½ in.
- Neck: 18¼ in.
- Chest and shoulders: 47½ in. normal and 51 in. expanded.
- Right shoulder joint: 21½ in.
- Left shoulder joint: 21¼ in.
- Biceps of right arm: 15½ in. straight and 16¾ in. flexed.
- Biceps of left arm: 14½ in. straight and 16½ in. flexed.
- Forearm, right: 13½ in.
- Forearm, left: 13¾ in.
- Right and left wrist: 7¾ in.
- Right and left thigh: 24¾ in.
- Calf: 15¼ in.
- Ankle: 9¼ in.

My best performances at the end of the six months which I spent with the hospitable doctor, in addition to those already mentioned, were as follows:

- I jerked a bar weighing 306 lb. with both hands.
- I pulled in clean to the shoulders a bar weighing 361 lb.
- I snatched a bar weighing 197½ lb. with the right hand (a world's record).

These feats were performed either in the Doctor's gymnasium or in Count Ribeaupierre's riding school and the weights were in every instance carefully checked. This reminds me of a humorous incident over which I have often laughed heartily. The doctor was at this time wearing a new pair of trousers, which fitted him exceedingly well, insomuch that I more than once expressed a wish to possess similar garments. Dr. von Krajewski jestingly replied, "My dear George, when you can beat Sandow's world's record of putting up 116 kilogrammes or 255½ lb. with one hand you shall have just such another pair!" It may have been this jest which spurred me on to make a special effort by putting up a weight of 122.25 kilogrammes (269½ lb. English). This was done in Count Ribeaupierre's private riding school, which was arranged for this occasion like a circus. The place was filled with a large audience of some of the most distinguished people in St. Petersburg. When I lifted this weight Dr. Krajewski in front of all the people rose from his seat, and lifted his hat to full arm's length above his head. I shall never forget the doctor on this occasion. His admiration for feats of strength was almost beyond understanding. Everybody was surprised by this evidence of his genuine emotion, and it seemed as though his enthusiasm spread itself over the whole of the audience, everybody congratulating me warmly. The doctor disappeared for a few minutes and returned with the promised pair of trousers. I don't mind admitting that, at the moment, I was almost more pleased with this gift than with the large gold Record Medal solemnly presented to me a few days later.

There was, indeed, something singular, I had almost said something mysterious, about Dr. von Krajewski. Something in the man's being seemed to melt in his love for feats of strength and agility, and flowed forth in an inexplicable fire on all artistes of this genre. These people often used to say to me, "We don't know how it is, but once the doctor appears on the scene one feels as though one had more strength." This was just the feeling I always had, but it surprised me to hear my impression confirmed by others. I went to Vienna in company with Dr. von Krajewski, and the pick of the St. Petersburg amateurs, Guido Meyer and Alexander von Schmelling. We were most hospitably received by the Vienna Athletic Club, and I made the acquaintance of various first-rate athletes and wrestlers.

It was there I first met Wilhelm Tiirck, a very strong man, at that time about forty years of age. He was nearly 6 ft. high and weighed 18 st. 12 lb. He could raise, largely by main force, a bar weighing 330 lb. to the full height of his arms, and could draw up a weight of 132 lb. in both hands simultaneously (264 lb. in all). My best performance at that time was 114 lb. in each hand, or 228 lb. in all. But in putting up a weight with one hand, which requires more skill, he could only manage 138½ lb. as against my 242 lb.

I may here point out that owing to the excitement attendant on such events it is very difficult for a man to do his best. My performances were:

- Jerking a bar with both hands, 311 lb.
- Slow pressing a bar with both hands, 249 lb.
- Slow pressing a bar with both hands, 220 lb., four times.

In weight-lifting, I was third, behind Tiirck and Binder, the latter also a Viennese athlete.

It seemed to me that the arrangement of the contests was all in favour of the Viennese, for even the very strong French champion, Pierre Bonnes, could not win a place, owing to the fact that the Viennese had, undoubtedly, been exclusively trained for these special feats. The same remark applies to the feats with separate weights (i.e., with the so-called short Bohlig dumb-bells). My fellow clubman, Meyer, it is true, made a very creditable show, but even he could not score much. Herr von Schmelling, a very tall man, 6 ft. 4½ in. in height and about 17 st. 4 lb. in weight, had wrestled with me and with Paul Pons for a full hour without decisive result, and was reckoned a better wrestler than I;

but he had very poor luck in Vienna, for, after defeating Wetasa, the best Viennese wrestler of that day, after a contest of one and a half hours, he had, owing to a misunderstanding with the umpire, to retire from a second contest with Burghardt. I was now Dr. von Krajewski's sole remaining hope in the wrestling bouts. I was in excellent fettle, and, first of all, threw several Viennese amateurs, in very quick time, less than one minute each. I was then matched with the Bavarian champion, Michael Hitzler, a wonderfully good wrestler, but rather too light a weight for me. I put out my full force and threw him after a plucky struggle lasting five minutes. It took me only two minutes to settle with Burghardt, who was not so good a man. I had now won the first prize in wrestling, the championship of Europe, a beautiful gold medal, and a magnificent championship belt. Dr. von Krajewski was delighted and congratulations rained down on me from every side.

WHAT WAS WRESTLING LIKE 120 YEARS AGO?

Wrestling had grown in popularity over the centuries. By the 1700s and 1800s, various wrestling styles had developed, and by the early 1900s, we find several distinct variants in the Western world worth differentiating:

- **Folk Wrestling Styles:** Rooted in farming communities, these styles were showcased in rural exhibitions and competitions. They focused primarily on throws and ground holds.

- **Greco-Roman Wrestling:** Despite its historical name, this style was created in 19th-century France. It features attacks above the waist, emphasizing throws and ground holds.

- **Freestyle Wrestling:** One of the Olympic wrestling styles, similar to Greco-Roman, but allowing attacks below the waist.

- **Catch-as-Catch-Can Wrestling:** Originating from rural England, this style was used in exhibitions, challenges, and festivals. With much more open rules, it allowed attacks below the waist and the use of holds and locks on the entire body. The catch-as-catch-can style developed several versions, largely due to the challenges of travel faced by rural communities in the United Kingdom. As a result, the United States absorbed influences from various migrant sources and wrestling variations from England, Scotland, and Ireland.

Professor Hueppe of Prague was one of the umpires in this competition. An enthusiast in gymnastics, he took a great interest in the wrestling contests and was good enough to praise me very highly. I received quite a general ovation at the supper given at the close of the contest, and the Athletic Club invited Dr. von Krajewski, Meyer von Schmelling and myself to a soirée.

Towards evening on the following day we found ourselves in the Club rooms, and the old doctor was the first to make himself at home and laid hold of the tools. Great surprise was shown on every side at seeing so old a man so keen at his work. He put up a bar of 154 lb. several times with two hands and performed a number of other feats of strength. Fired by his example, I achieved the following performance: lying on the ground I raised above the head and put up 331½ lb.

Next day, on the invitation of one of the umpires, Herr Victor Silberer, we made an excursion to this gentleman's country house on the Semmering Pass, and spent a most enjoyable time.

Herr Silberer was the proprietor and editor of the Allgemeine Sport Zeitung, and himself a keen sportsman. After our return to St. Petersburg I was challenged on various pretexts by Wetasa of Vienna and also by Lurich to wrestle for the championship of Europe or to defend the same. Dr. von Krajewski undertook the preliminaries, but both men sought to insist on such impossible conditions that the contest fell through. Even at that date I had not the slightest fear of either of them, Wetasa was already somewhat past his prime, while I knew that Lurich, though somewhat more experienced, was a weaker wrestler than myself.

I spent the remainder of the year at Dr. von Krajewski's, and in January, 1899, after a keen struggle won the championship of Finland from twenty competitors.

Although from the date of my first great success in the wrestling ring onwards I trained less and less for weight-lifting records, yet in January, 1899, I pressed a bar of 279¾ lb. with both hands.

The time for my enrolment in the army had now arrived, and I was commanded to join the Preobrazhensky Polk (the 1st Life Guards of the Czar), but was released from service after five months. On May 16, in Count Ribeaupierre's riding school, I wrestled to a finish the contest with Herr von Schmelling which had been left undecided in the previous year, and defeated him in twenty-five minutes by means of a "half-nelson," thus winning the championship for 1898. A few days later, on May 19, a second victory over Schmelling in forty-four minutes gained me the Russian championship for 1899. Schmelling was one of my toughest opponents!

After this, I again trained for some time at weight-lifting and made some progress, as I jerked a bar of 330 lb. with both hands; but in trying to slow press 286 lb. with one hand, I strained a sinew in my right shoulder, an injury which was destined to trouble me for years afterwards. At first I thought little of this trifling pain and trained for the Championship of the World wrestling contests in Paris, which took place in November. I was firmly resolved to become a professional wrestler. Although my arm had not yet fully recovered I went to Paris and took part in the contests.

THE "BLOOD SPORTS" OF THE ERA

When we read about matches featuring multiethnic wrestlers from around the world, the image of a "great white dragon" showdown or a "Street Fighter"-style clash immediately comes to mind. In fact, these ancient and real encounters, like those described in this book, served as inspiration for such pop culture platforms and their development of characters.

While most wrestlers were European—primarily German, French, and Italian—others hailed from the Netherlands, Switzerland, Hungary, Denmark, Belgium, Austria, and Russia. The roster was further enriched by "exotic" wrestlers, as they were known in the Western world of the time, including Africans, Turks, Indians, and Japanese competitors.

North American wrestlers rarely entered this equation due to the challenges of distance and the high costs involved in organizing these matches. Additionally, the particular style of wrestling derived from Catch-As-Catch-Can often did not align with the rules used in European competitions.

The list of competitors for this tournament was as follows: Charles le Meunier (France), Henri Pechon (France), Francois le Farinier (Swiss), Feriol Marius (France), Henri Alphonse (Swiss), Loir dit Porthos, Trillat le Savoyard, Capitant le Parisien, Louis Chappe (all of France), Niemann (Germany), Camillus Evertsen (Denmark), Pietro Dalmasso (Italy), Barnet le Déménageur (France), Jaccavail (France), Devaux (Belgium), Dirk van den Berg (Holland), Raoul le Boucher (France), Raymond Franc (France), Victor Delmas (France), Edgar Joly (France), Hautier le Breton, Leon le Jouteur (France), Bonera Domenico (Italy), Aimable de la Calmette (France), Starck (Germany), Jean le Marseillais (France), Edouard Robin (France), Jax le Taureau (France), Henri Lorange (France), Fengler (Germany), Alis-Amba (Africa), Eberle (Germany), Robinet (France), Laurent le Beaucairois (France), Constant le Boucher (Belgium), Kara Ahmed (Turkey), Charles Poirée (France), Peyrousse (France), Miller (Germany), Paul Pons (France), besides myself.

My first opponent was a medium wrestler, Loir, nicknamed Porthos. I got him down in eighteen seconds! My second was a Frenchman from the South, named Robinet, a wrestler with a fairly good style and till then of fairly high reputation. It is, perhaps, only natural that foreign wrestlers should be greeted with a certain amount of distrust. I was at that time almost unknown to the general public in France, and everyone was astonished to see me defeat the popular Robinet in the short space of four minutes. Robinet was too sportsmanlike to attribute his defeat to accident, but, in answer to questions, said that I was very strong; "he has a grip like a vice, and if he gets you on the ground you are done for". It was about this time that people began to call me "the Russian Lion."

After the struggle with Robinet, the next morning I went to the Gymnasium Piaza, Rue Faubourg St. Denis, to train, when Leon Dumont, the French wrestler, put my shoulder out of joint, and for a long time my right arm seemed half paralyzed. Monsieur Piaza used hot and cold shower-baths and electricity to try to restore the use of my arm, but with little result.

It has long been the custom in wrestling circles to put all sorts of difficulties in the way of beginners who threaten to prove dangerous rivals later on, and thus to scare the newcomers out of the profession. I myself was told that "Beginners who may become dangerous must be defeated often and severely in order to get rid of them."

In accordance with this policy the third opponent assigned to me was one of the best French wrestlers, the versatile Aimable de la Calmette. This athlete, as I soon discovered, was not nearly so strong as I, but far more experienced, a fact which made it necessary for me to be careful, for an experienced wrestler is far more dangerous than one who is merely strong. One is never safe from surprises, and it is almost impossible to calculate what such wrestlers may do. Well, I threw the worthy Aimable after forty-seven minutes, but learned a great deal in the course of this struggle. On the following day Laurent le Beaucairois, a very strong and clever performer, appeared upon the scene. Till then I had

FRANZ BIENKOWSKI, "CYCLOPS"

Opolskie, Poland [1862-1924].

Coming from a family of blacksmiths with a naturally large and robust physique, Bienkowski was accustomed to hard labor from an early age. His natural strength and imposing physical stature made him well-known in his region. Together with Charles A. Sampson, he formed a successful duo that toured Europe, England, the United States, and Canada, performing feats of strength in circuses and theaters. Sampson and Cyclops are considered "archetypes" of the Vaudeville Theater Strongman.

not believed it possible that so corpulent a man—Laurent weighed 18 st. 12 lb., though he was slightly shorter than I—could show so much activity and nimbleness. Laurent was an old hand at the game, having wrestled for fifteen years, and it did not look as if there was much chance for me, who had scarcely had fifteen months' experience. In strength I was the Frenchman's equal, if not his superior, and I made up my mind to be on my guard and give no chances. We wrestled for thirty minutes, when the referee declared the contest a draw.

After this last bout, the weakness in my arm gave me a good deal of trouble, and I thought it best to retire from the tournament, especially as a French surgeon had ordered me to avoid all overstraining for twelve months. I sincerely wish that I had followed his advice!

I looked on at a few more contests and then returned home to have my arm seen to, going in for treatment with electricity for about six months, but I am inclined to fancy that this did me more harm than good. All went well, and in May, 1900, I again began to lift heavy weights.

ANCIENT MEDICAL TREATMENTS

Excess and negligence in training are not exclusive to modern times. Even in Hack's era, without a deep understanding of training physiology and regenerative processes, injuries of all kinds occurred.

In this book, we find classic recommendations that seemed to have faded over time but resurfaced with vigor during the COVID-19 era: adequate rest, sun exposure, breathing fresh air, strength and mobility training, and avoiding "drugs" (both legal and illegal), such as tobacco and alcohol.

Specifically, in the biographical chapter, we encounter treatments involving hot-cold contrasts, which are still used today to reduce inflammation, alleviate pain, and improve circulation. Electrical treatments, particularly galvanism, were also employed as therapy. At the time, it was believed to be a potential cure for certain ailments. However, in Hack's case, and specifically for his shoulder injury, these methods proved largely ineffective, as was the case with many treatments of that era.

With the thoughtlessness of youth, I soon began to lift the heaviest bars again, and my arm, which had scarcely recovered, was again injured in an attempt to establish fresh records in weight-lifting. Dr. von Krajewski warned me seriously, and I grew more prudent and avoided tours de force of this nature.

In June, 1900, a wrestling combat took place at Moscow. This was my first appearance as a professional wrestler. The tournament lasted forty days, my salary being 2,500 francs (or £100) per month. We were wrestling for two prizes, viz., the championships of St. Petersburg and of Moscow. As I succeeded in winning both, I gained another 1,500 fr. for the St. Petersburg championship and 2,500 fr. more, being the amount of the first Moscow prize. I met Aimable and Petroff, and defeated them. I also threw the eel-like Constant le Boucher, a young Belgian, in five minutes. Petroff was an immensely strong Bulgarian. Constant was incredibly clever and agile, but seemed to undervalue me as an opponent. As he admitted afterwards, he had heard me described as being somewhat clumsy, though very strong. After defeating Constant, the French wrestlers put Peyrousse forward against me. This wrestler was tremendously powerful, but had little heart, so that hardly had we commenced struggling than he practically threw himself, greatly to the surprise of his compatriots, who had counted on his crushing me. My second bout with him lasted only seven seconds. Following Peyrousse I met and defeated an enormously strong Cossack in Michailoff, whom I threw in ten minutes. While our championship matches in Moscow were still proceeding, a great wrestling competition had already commenced in Vienna. Unfortunately, I entered too late and did not reach Vienna until the final stages were in progress. My old opponent Pons took first prize. Kara Ahmed, a first-rate Turkish wrestler, was second, and the corpulent Laurent third. Neither Pons nor the Turk would consent to meet me. Apparently, they were in no hurry to risk their freshly-won laurels. The good-natured Laurent alone was willing to wrestle a fall with me.

I first of all had a bout with a very tall and heavy Spaniard, named Chorella, whom I threw in the short space of twenty-nine seconds. I had more trouble with a Dutchman, Dirk van den Berg, a finely built athlete. Van den Berg played a defensive game, looking out for some oversight on my part, but at length I defeated him in twenty-two minutes. I found an even more wily opponent in the German Fengler, who seemed a good-natured man and made all sorts of proposals to me before the contest, but once we set to work, I found that he was only too anxious to beat me. I now began to realize that in order to win one requires not only brute strength but must also employ, in a far greater degree than the uninitiated would suppose, both judgment and reflection. I threw Fengler in twenty-six minutes. On the next day, I wrestled with the doughty and corpulent Laurent le Beaucairois. We had a pretty lively set-to, and the Frenchman let it clearly be seen that he had no hope of beating me, for at the end of an hour, he withdrew from the contest. Early in September, I went to Dresden, the capital of Saxony, to attend a small wrestling competition. I was the chief attraction there and wrestled almost nightly with from three to five opponents, nearly all of whom I defeated very quickly, e.g. :

Winzer of Hamburg in seven minutes.
The Austrian Burghardt in six minutes.
And the two nimble Italian brothers, Emilio and Giovanni Raicevich, in three and six minutes respectively, all in a single evening!

I threw Fengler and Konietzko on another evening in three minutes altogether. At Dresden, I met a very stout and heavy wrestler named Sebastian Miller. This worthy man weighed nearly 24 st., and was fairly strong, but so deficient in science that I threw him in three minutes, and immediately afterward, a nimble but smaller Frenchman named Maurice Gambier in five minutes, and Hitzler in twenty-three minutes. Hitzler had improved greatly. I took the first prize at Dresden.

From Dresden I went to Chemnitz, another Saxon town of somewhat less than a quarter of a million inhabitants. Here the contestants were: Gambier (France), Hofer (Germany), Seb Miller (Germany), Konietzko (Germany), Buisson (France), Hitzler (Germany), Winzer (Germany), Giovanni and Emilio Raicevich (Italy), Rossner (Germany), Petri (Holland), Oscar Uhlig (Germany), Burghardt (Austria), Diriks (Belgium), and myself. At Chemnitz, I, for the first time, met my old antagonist Lurich. As often happens, the management of another theatre, in order to compete with our undertaking, had engaged Lurich and a number of other inferior wrestlers. Lurich went about boasting loudly that he had more than once defeated me with ease. His impresario billed Lurich as the strongest man in the world and "the invincible wrestler."

WLADYSLAW PYTLASINSKI

Warsaw, Poland [1863-1933]

Ladislaus Pytlasinski was a Polish wrestler, world champion, and coach. Known as "The Father of Polish Wrestling", he played a pivotal role in developing the sport in Poland.
The son of a butcher, Pytlasinski worked as a mechanic by trade. During the January Uprising—a conflict between Poland and Tsarist Russia—he fled to Switzerland, where he began his wrestling career.

Specializing in Greco-Roman wrestling while incorporating elements of freestyle, he was renowned for his exceptional physical condition. Pytlasinski enjoyed an illustrious wrestling career, winning 794 out of 800 professional matches. He claimed victory in the prestigious Paris World Wrestling Championship in 1898, 1899, and 1900.
In 1918, following Poland's regained independence, Pytlasinski returned to his homeland and donated all his gold medals and trophies to the National Treasury, earning him the "Cross of Merit". He later became the commander of the Civil Guard and Chief of Criminal Police in Warsaw.

He began training police forces in wrestling and self-defense while organizing amateur tournaments. In 1922, Pytlasinski founded the Polish Athletic Society, which eventually became part of the International Wrestling Federation.
Pytlasinski authored two books: Secrets of Wrestling (1929) and Weightlifting (1930). The former, aimed at wrestling enthusiasts, outlined methods for training muscles, improving joint function, and enhancing nerves, heart, and lung health. The latter focused on weightlifting training principles.

Though as a rule I have no great liking for impromptu challenges, yet in view of this continuous and brazen puffing of Lurich I could not refrain from challenging him to a wrestling match when I found that he persisted in these wanton personal attacks upon me. Accordingly, Hitzler and I strolled around one evening—it was Monday, September 17—to the theatre at which Lurich was engaged and offered to wrestle with him. Although Lurich had declared himself ready to meet any wrestler, amateur or professional, who chose to come forward, our challenge was not accepted, on the plea that the "invincible" had already his full quota of opponents. It was nevertheless announced from the stage that Herr Lurich would wrestle with Hackenschmidt on the following Wednesday.

On the appointed evening we were punctually in our places, but we noticed that Lurich was already provided with two opponents. One of these, who seemed to be quite ignorant of wrestling, he threw in less than a minute. He then prepared to serve his second opponent in similar fashion when this latter suddenly vanished from the stage, crying out as he went, "Yonder stands Herr Hackenschmidt" (pointing at me), "he will take my place, as I don't feel well". I went on to the stage, amid thunderous applause from the crowded audience which had assembled, in order to wrestle with Lurich. But no sooner did the "invincible wrestler" catch sight of me than he turned deadly pale and bolted into the wings, and in spite of repeated calls, he absolutely declined to return. The Chemnitz Allgemeine Zeitung (No. 29 of September 21, 1900) printed the following note on this incident:

"As our readers are aware, George Lurich, who describes himself as the 'Champion Athlete of the World' and 'Strongest Man in the World,' has for some days past been appearing at the Mosella Saal. In addition to a somewhat glowing advertisement of his powers, he has issued on his bills, etc., etc., a challenge to all wrestlers, whether amateur or professional. On Monday evening George Hackenschmidt, who is taking part in a wrestling competition at the Kaufmannische Vereinshaus, challenged him to a wrestling bout on Wednesday evening. News of this spread very quickly among all the sporting elements of Chemnitz, with the result that the Mosella Saal was packed from floor to ceiling on the evening in question. Everyone looked forward with impatience for the beginning of the wrestling match. The disappointment of the spectators can therefore be imagined, when Herr Lurich appeared on the stage in the company of Herr Gleissner of Borna and another gentleman of whose identity we are ignorant. To dispose of a wrestler like Herr Gleissner was, of course, mere child's play for Herr Lurich. The second wrestler retired in favor of Herr Hackenschmidt, whose challenge had been given on Monday evening, and who therefore had the prior claim. Hereupon the curtain was abruptly lowered amid stormy scenes on the part of the indignant audience. Cries of 'Come out!' 'Shame!' 'Swindle!' were quickly heard, mingled with whistling and cat-calls enough to make one's flesh creep. All this was directed against the 'invincible' Herr Lurich, who, we are informed, has caused similar scandals in other towns, such as Elberfeld, where the competitors in the International Wrestling Contests were unfortunately prevented by the terms of their engagement from exposing the Russian in the manner adopted on Wednesday. Even the management of the Mosella Saal failed to persuade Lurich to meet Hackenschmidt.

Presumably Lurich will not be allowed to appear again until he has wrestled with Hackenschmidt, who is ready to meet him on any evening."

Lurich left Chemnitz on the following morning.

My sole object in recording this unpleasant incident is to enable the English public to estimate at their true value the insinuations directed against me by a fellow countryman in the summer of 1904. We continued our tournament at Chemnitz undisturbed, and in addition to winning first prize, I received a splendid ovation from the public, Hitzler and Gambier gaining second and third prizes respectively. From Chemnitz, I journeyed to Buda Pesth, the beautiful capital of Hungary, where a wrestling contest had commenced on September 24. The participants were: Kara Ahmed (Turkey), Robinet (France), Muldoon (of America, but not the celebrated Physical Culturist), Charles (France), Krendel (Austria), Weber (Germany), Hitzler (Germany), Celestin Moret (France), Lassartesse (France), Ignace Nollys (Belgium), Albert de Paris (France), Giovanni Raicevich (Italy), Pibius (France), Burghardt (Austria), Mayer (Hungary), Sandorfi (Hungary), and Aimable (France), etc.

One of my first opponents was Robinet, who was a great favorite with the Buda Pesth public, on the strength of his performances some years previously. I threw the Frenchman in eight minutes, and, later on in the competition, I defeated Albert de Paris, a very clever wrestler, in five minutes; Weber, of Germany, in two minutes; Aimable in twenty-five minutes; and Van den Berg in twenty-four minutes. My severest bout was with the Turk, Kara Ahmed, whom it took me nearly three hours to defeat. But never, while I live, shall I forget what then took place. The whole audience rose like one man, and thunders of applause echoed through the building. I was seized, carried shoulder-high, and decked with flowers. For fully a quarter of an hour I was borne like a victorious general through the streets, kissed, embraced, etc. I can assure you I was heartily glad when I at last made my escape to the privacy of the dressing room. Never, even in Paris, have I experienced a similar ovation. I am not likely to forget those worthy Hungarians.

The result was as follows: I won the first prize of 1,500 kronen besides my salary, the second prize of 1,000 kronen going to Kara Ahmed, and the third of 600 kronen to Dirk van den Berg, and the fourth of 400 kronen to Aimable de la Calmette.

We left the hospitable walls of Buda Pesth, and I next won the first prize at Graz, in Steiermark. None of the contests there were of great importance. At Graz, I was pitted against the German athlete Rasso, an exceedingly powerful man, but no wrestler. I threw him as I pleased, clean and cleverly in five minutes, to the great surprise of the good people of Graz, who were familiar with Rasso's Herculean feats as an athlete.

Towards the end of October, I gained a first prize at Nürnberg, a prominent city of Bavaria, after which I returned to St. Petersburg, as my arm had again become almost useless owing to the continual strain to which it had been subjected. After eight weeks' rest, during which my arm underwent thorough treatment, my ambition again drove me to Paris in order to wrestle matches with Pons, Beaucairois, Constant, Van den Berg, and Aimable.

I twice defeated Aimable, once in thirty-four and once in seventeen minutes. Van den Berg I threw in twenty-five and in three minutes. My first bout with Constant lasted an hour without result, and then we wrestled for two hours and a quarter, when he was declared the loser. Pons avoided meeting me. But Beaucairois, who must have known that I was suffering from a sharp attack of influenza, ventured to try his luck with me. I defeated him in twenty minutes, and then, in spite of my ailing condition, wrestled for an hour without result, and at the end of the day, in defiance of my doctor's advice, I again began to wrestle with the doughty Laurent. Half unconscious owing to the fever which coursed through my veins, after a struggle of twenty-three minutes, I fell a victim to a bras roulé of the Frenchman's.

This was, strictly speaking, the first fall I had incurred in the course of my otherwise victorious career as a professional wrestler, and it was entirely due to my pride, since the Paris doctor called it inexcusable on my part to think of wrestling in such a condition!

THE "TURKISH INVASION"

It is common to hear about the presence of Turkish wrestlers during this period. Historically, Turkey (then the Ottoman Empire) was home to exceptional wrestlers with a tradition and culture of wrestling that had been developing for centuries. The Kırkpınar tournament, held in Edirne, is a prime example of this legacy—a practice that has endured through time and fostered a tradition of skilled wrestlers.

The term "Turkish Invasion" was a sensationalized headline used in 1894 when the French wrestler Doublier visited Turkey to recruit the best wrestlers to face Europeans. Among these wrestlers were Kara Osman,

Nurullah, and Youssuf Ismael (mentioned in the Masters of Strength section). Youssuf, known as "The Terrible Turk", experienced tremendous success in France for three years and later in the United States.

The so-called "Turkish Invasion" was part of a broader trend at the time—international competitions designed to draw larger audiences. Unfortunately, it was common during this era to label many non-European wrestlers as "Turkish", even when they were, in fact, Bulgarian, Persian, Indian, or African.

I had scarcely recovered when I had to fulfill an engagement in Hamburg, where the following wrestlers were engaged in a tournament: Max Nirsche (Berlin), Strenge (Berlin), Tom Clayton "Bulldog" (England), Joe Carroll (England), Lassartesse (France), Branken (Holland), Giovanni Raicevich (Italy), Celestin Moret (France), Weber (Germany), Saurer (Bavaria), G. Lurich (Russia), Pietro le Belge (Belgium), G. Semmel (Hamburg), Constant le Boucher (Belgium), G. Jeurisson (Belgium), Emil Bau (Germany), H. Landy (Holland), H. Oehlers (Hamburg), Kara Mustapha (Turkey), Clement le Terrassier (Belgium), Hitzler (Bavaria), Poirée (France), Kreindl (Austria), Peyrousse (France), Jess Pedersen (Denmark), Lemmertz (Germany), Winzer (Hamburg), Hassan Omer (Turkey), Orondi (Steiermark), Dirk van den Berg (Holland), Diriks (Belgium), P. Belling (Berlin), H. Eberle (Germany), and Halil Adali, undoubtedly the best wrestler Turkey has ever produced.

I first wrestled with some less important men and then beat Orondi in ten seconds, Lemmertz in less than two minutes, Diriks in 1 min. 32 sec., and Belling in less than twenty minutes. Jess Pedersen (Denmark) in twenty minutes, and Van den Berg. I next engaged the German champion, Eberle, a very strong and accomplished wrestler, who gave up the struggle at the end of twenty minutes. This did not please the audience, and led to a scene of wild disorder. The police were called in and they put a stop to the whole tournament. There was nothing left for us but to start for home, which I accordingly did without having wrestled with Halil Adali.

Then on March 14, 1901, came a bolt from the blue in the shape of a telegram informing me that Dr. Krajewski was dead. But a little time before I had seen the worthy doctor in the best of health, and I now learned that he had succumbed to apoplexy, after having been so unlucky as to fall and break a leg on the Fontanka Bridge on the Newski Prospekt. I, in common with all other Russian athletes, shed many a tear over the loss of this noble-hearted gentleman. In him, I lost a friend who was almost a second father.

Towards the end of March, another wrestling contest was held in St. Petersburg. Amongst others, I defeated the strong and nimble French wrestler,

Lassartesse, in twenty minutes and Petroff in seven minutes, by an arm-roll or bras roulé, obtaining the first prize, a gold medal.

At Easter of this year (1901), the wrestling contest for the championship of the world began in Vienna. This championship I consider the biggest I ever gained since never before nor since has such a wonderful array of contestants been gathered together. There were, from Germany, Jacobus Koch, H. Eberle, Stark, Axa, Missbach, and Hitzler; from Belgium, Omer de Bouillon and Clement le Terrassier; from Holland, Dirk van den Berg; from Italy, G. Raicevich and Figini; from Turkey, Kara Ahmed, Halil Adali, and Coord Derelli; from Denmark, Jess Pedersen; from America, John Piening; from Austria, Franzel, Sporer, Kreindl, and Sprecht; from France, Paul Pons, Laurent le Beaucairois, Aimable de la Calmette, and a whole host of lesser lights. Among others, I defeated Omer de Bouillon, a most excellent Belgian wrestler, in nine minutes, and Hitzler in twelve minutes. It was here that the small but nimble Bayer caused such general astonishment by throwing the gigantic Turk, Halil Adali (who was 6 ft. 2½ in. in height and weighed 20 st. 5 lb.), in a minute and a half, taking him by surprise with a brilliant bras roulé. Here, I made the acquaintance of a German wrestler named Koch, who was, I think, the best German wrestler I have ever seen. He was very strong and decidedly clever but did not do much in Vienna on this occasion, as he was not in particularly good form. I threw him in twenty minutes. I had heard a great deal of the American wrestler Piening, who recently sought notoriety in England by appearing against me. But he, too, though an excellent, if not particularly powerful, wrestler, could do but little in Vienna. Pons, Adali, Laurent, and I were rather too good for him. I threw Piening in thirty-one seconds! Beaucairois fell in forty-one minutes, and Pons, in spite of a stubborn defense, in seventy-nine minutes. I had a pretty tough job with the tall Frenchman (6 ft. 4½ in. in height and weighing over 18 st.), and my victory was greeted with generous applause. The Turk Halil Adali, whom I consider the best of all my opponents, was even stronger than Pons. Adali possessed gigantic strength and staying power, but I was in pretty good form. On the first day, after wrestling for an hour and eighteen minutes, we drew. The next day, after a contest of forty minutes, the Turk gave in, being convinced that

I must win. Indeed, I had wrestled in first-rate form and had reduced the good man to a somewhat demoralized condition. The results came out as follows: Hackenschmidt, 1; Adali, 2; Pons, 3; etc.

From Vienna, I went to Stettin, where I took first prize in a minor contest. In the middle of May, a great wrestling contest was held in Berlin, and a number of excellent wrestlers were engaged, Lurich among others. There were two classes in this contest: Lightweights (85 kg. or 13 st. 5 lb. and under) and Heavyweights (85 kg. or 13 st. 5 lb. and over). Consequently, on this occasion, I did not meet Lurich, his weight at that time being 13 st. 4 lb. I was, however, somewhat astonished to find that, on being matched against Piening (whom I threw in thirty-one seconds in Vienna), he twice wrestled with him for an hour, the result being a draw in each case!

I again threw Koch (in seven minutes) and several Berlin wrestlers in a few seconds, but in a contest with Pedersen, which I undertook by the express desire of the management, I drew after a two-hour struggle. The whole contest was broken off owing to the failure of the management. The best wrestlers, including Petroff, Hitzler, Pohl, Pons, Pedersen, and myself, continued the contest at the Metropole Theatre in Berlin. I now threw Hitzler in twenty-four minutes, Petroff in thirty-one minutes, and Pedersen in twenty-nine minutes. The German wrestler, Pohl, who finished second and was left in the final heat with Pons and myself, was a new opponent to me. Pohl was very strong and clever. He threw Pedersen in three minutes. I defeated him in thirteen minutes after an indecisive struggle of one hour on the previous evening. The periodical Sport im Bild commented on this match, in which it was generally thought that Pohl would prove a dangerous opponent, as follows: "It was apparent from the very beginning of the final round (Hackenschmidt v. Pohl) that Hackenschmidt was in deadly earnest and anxious to bring matters to a crisis as soon as possible. Seizing Pohl round the body with irresistible force, he endeavored again and again to bring him to the ground, till at last he succeeded in doing so, though only at the cost of tremendous exertion. It then became clear that the Russian was resting for a moment and calling up a fresh reserve of strength, for he held Pohl motionless on the ground for some time. Then followed a sudden and violent ceinture de côté, from the left, to which Pohl nearly fell a victim. With one hand, Hackenschmidt nearly jerked him onto his back. Then followed one or two remassements by means of which the Russian forced his opponent's head onto the ground, then another ceinture, which, however, failed to bring about the desired result. The struggle had lasted thirteen minutes when Hackenschmidt at last secured the grip he so frequently employs with success. With his left hand, he jerked Pohl so energetically that, in spite of his great weight (110 kg. or 17 st. 4 lb.), the Hamburg champion fell fair and square on both shoulders. The whole character of the contest—in which Hackenschmidt attacked throughout while Pohl remained on the defensive—proved conclusively that the Russian is greatly his superior in strength".

I wrestled with Pons, but at the end of the bout, the Frenchman retired; after being twice within an ace of defeat, he was unable to continue owing to an accident to his arm. I was awarded first prize amid deafening applause and received a gigantic laurel wreath nearly 6 ft. in diameter.

I spent a very pleasant time in Berlin and there made the acquaintance of the celebrated sculptor, Professor Reinhold Begas, who asked me to sit for him in the character of "Prometheus Vinctus." Professor Begas, a stately old man who carried his seventy years well, took a great interest in wrestling and was nearly always present during our contests.

I now returned home to rest and underwent several courses of treatment to benefit my arm, the most successful of these being the Priessnitz cold-water pack. The measurement of my biceps, which had decreased to 15½ in., rose again to 17½ in., and my weight increased from 14 st. 2 lb. to 15 st. 6 lb. After three months, in October 1901, I was able to take up wrestling again in Moscow. I was in excellent form, and, among other events, I threw Lassartesse in seven minutes, Hitzler in twenty-one minutes, and the young Frenchman Raoul le Boucher—a very powerful, heavy, and skillful wrestler (6 ft. 2½ in. in height and weighing 19 st. 9 lb.)—in twenty-three minutes, despite his furious resistance. I also defeated five excellent Moscow amateurs in seven minutes! This last tour de force I repeated shortly afterward—at the end of October— in Munich, where I defeated five professional wrestlers also in seven minutes.

Among others, I beat Burghardt (Austria) in six minutes, Cassino (France) in thirty seconds, Hitzler in twenty-three minutes, Rédel in twenty-seven seconds, Blatte (of Munich) in two and a half minutes, Eigemann (from Elberfeld) in less than one minute, Marchand (the Frenchman) in two minutes, and Koch in twenty-five minutes.

I was next matched for the second time against the German champion, Eberle, who was now in better form than he had been at Hamburg. I was prepared for a fairly long struggle in case he adopted defensive tactics, but to my surprise, Eberle took the offensive against me. I allowed him to take the lower hold from behind, and as I tightened this by a sturdy swing of the leg, I got him off his balance. He fell, and I quickly turned him on his back. To the astonishment of everyone, especially Eberle himself, the whole contest lasted only five minutes.

YUSUF ISMAIL

Shumen, Ottoman Empire (modern-day Bulgaria) [1857–1898].

Youssuf Ismael, known as "The Terrible Turk", was a wrestler who competed in Europe and the United States. Famous for his enormous size and incredible strength, he was the undefeated European champion from 1894 to 1898 and a key figure in the so-called "Turkish Invasion". He also earned the title of North American Heavyweight Champion in 1908. The Terrible Turk met a tragic end. On his return to his homeland, carrying the fortune he had amassed as a professional wrestler in the United States, converted into gold, the ship he was on sank. According to legend, the weight of his fortune prevented him from swimming to safety, and he disappeared into the depths of the ocean.

On the following day, in the company of other wrestlers, I paid a visit to "Steierer Hans," a great character in Munich. In his earlier days, he had traveled the world in the role of Hercules and had been unsurpassed in lifting weights with one finger. The worthy soul had now settled down as an innkeeper. In an underground room, he had a museum consisting chiefly of shapeless stones, axle-trees, and weights, with which he performed various tricks for our entertainment, accompanied by amusing commentary. Just for fun, I lifted with one hand a stone with weights attached, the entire load weighing 660 lb. In November, a small contest took place at Elberfeld, where I was once again an easy winner.

On November 30, 1901, a contest for the wrestling championship of the world commenced at the Casino de Paris. I had entered for this, and before it began, at an independent performance, I threw five professional wrestlers in six minutes altogether. For this tournament, some 130 wrestlers had entered.

Among others, I defeated Mario in three minutes and Buisson in three and three-quarter minutes. My first important adversary was Alexandre le Marseillais, a tall and heavy (17 st. 11 lb.), yet accomplished wrestler, whom I threw after a severe struggle of twenty minutes. I wrestled for one hour without result with Omer de Bouillon, who was in excellent form, but I defeated him the following day in twenty minutes. I next threw Koch in twenty minutes, Maurice Gambier in a short two minutes, Emile Vervet in six minutes, and the Frenchman Raoul le Boucher in twenty-one minutes. Raoul wrestled somewhat savagely, but this did not avail him much as I turned him with a "half-nelson" and pinned both his shoulders to the ground.

At last, my time came to wrestle with the celebrated Belgian, Constant le Boucher, in the final contest. On this particular evening, I happened to be in good form and as cool as ice. I secured a splendid grip and, to everyone's surprise, managed to throw the Belgian after only eight minutes of wrestling. This was on December 19, 1901. I received a magnificent ovation, and the newspapers devoted whole columns of space to me. On December 27, I wrestled again with Constant and was declared the winner after a long struggle.

The final results of the tournament were as follows:

- First prize (two gold medals and 3,000 francs): Hackenschmidt (one gold medal for defeating all four lightweight champions, the other for beating the heavyweights).
- Second prize (a gold and silver medal, and 1,750 francs): Constant le Boucher.
- Third prize (700 francs): Omer de Bouillon.
- Fourth prize (450 francs): Raoul le Boucher.
- Fifth prize (300 francs): Hitzler.
- Sixth prize (200 francs): Emil Vervet.

By mid-January, I felt it was high time to avail myself of an invitation to stay at Alsleben in Germany from Herr Siebert, the trainer, as my health had begun to suffer from my severe exertions during the championship contest. My weight had decreased to 14 st. 6 lb.

WHAT WERE COMPETITIONS LIKE?

From the information available, it's clear that wrestling matches were major sporting events, comparable in proportional magnitude to modern-day UFC or WWE events. These matches were not staged or choreographed. While some might assume they were akin to the scripted pantomimes of contemporary wrestling entertainment, these contests were taken very seriously.

For one, they had no time limits. Many of the accounts in this book describe matches lasting between 20 and 40 minutes, with some extending up to three hours! These events took place in pubs, theaters, and even stadiums when the occasion warranted it.

The rise of wrestling during this period can be attributed to significant changes in both participants and spectators. With the economic shifts of the new century, audiences became more consumer-oriented. This development led to wrestling becoming a true spectacle, particularly in Great Britain, where it gained extensive coverage from the press of the time.

At Alsleben, a quiet little country town, I was able to give my nerves a thorough rest. Wrestling had become abhorrent to me after hastening from one tournament to another. I was tired of the arena, especially as my arm grew more painful by the day.

Herr Siebert, a man of great experience, advised me strongly to wait until I had fully recovered my health and taken a thorough rest before making any rash decisions. Thanks to the quiet and good care, I recovered remarkably well and gradually began to train under Siebert's guidance with weights and dumbbells.

On January 27, I established a new world record by raising a weight of 187 lb. beyond my back with bent knees. Not long after, for a wager, I jumped 100 times over a table with my feet close together. My former depression gave way to vitality and the pleasures of life.

While staying with Siebert, I established two new world records:

1. 110 lb. lifted fifty times with bent knees

2. 110 lb. in the right hand and 100 lb. in the left hand held out simultaneously at arm's length but improved this afterwards to 110 and 100

lb. respectively.

About this time my patron, Count Ribeaupierre, wrote to me from St. Petersburg suggesting that I should enter into an agreement with Herr Delmer, of Brussels, proprietor of the "Biceps." I had already an engagement with Herr Delmer, having consented to take part in a wrestling competition in Belgium, but had been prevented by ill-health from keeping my promise. I wrote to Herr Delmer. We soon came to an understanding, and now, restored to health and strength, I quitted Herr Siebert's hospitable roof, once more a wrestler heart and soul!

Early in 1902, I arrived in England to challenge any available opponents. Wrestling had yet to gain much popularity in Britain, especially in the Greco-Roman style. Few first-class exponents of this method had visited the country.

About this time, an American wrestler named Carkeek made his appearance in London. I had known this man in France as an average wrestler. He was about forty years of age and claimed, among other things, to have defeated Beaucairois, Gambier, and Pytlasinski. I sent more than one challenge to his manager and also to Carkeek himself, but they were invariably refused. I was on the point of leaving England when it came to my knowledge that Carkeek, believing me to have already gone, had challenged any professional wrestler then in London to wrestle with him either in the Greco-Roman, "Catch-as-catch-can," or Cornish styles, and would be sure to make a big advertisement out of my departure. I therefore purchased a box close to the stage (of the Alhambra), and as soon as Carkeek had finished his challenge, I sprang, accompanied by Mr. Vansittart, the famous athlete, known as "The Man with the Grip of Iron," onto the stage in full wrestling costume, while my companion, holding a stake of £25 in his hand, challenged Carkeek to wrestle with me, and undertook to hand over the sum he held if I failed to throw Carkeek at least ten times within an hour. A tremendous uproar ensued, and, though the audience took our part, we were compelled to leave the stage by the police. On the following day, I lodged £25 with the editor of the Sportsman on the conditions already announced from the stage. All the newspapers gave favorable notices of my debut, and on March 10, I received an engagement at the Tivoli Theatre, London. For some time, my health suffered from a climate to which I was unaccustomed, but I nevertheless accepted further engagements, which were freely offered me.

In order to have a useful opponent for training purposes, I summoned my friend Koch from Germany, and we wrestled together almost every day for practice, wrestling continually for some months and defeating all opponents. Then I made the acquaintance of Tom Cannon, the well-known wrestler, who lived in Liverpool, and only wrestled occasionally.

At the end of July, Koch and I left England for the Continent and engaged in tournaments at Brussels, Liège, Namur, and other places, in all of which I won the first prize, Koch generally succeeding in winning the second.

THE GREAT GAMA

Amritsar, Punjab, British India (now Pakistan) [1878-1960].

The Great Gama was a renowned wrestler in the traditional Pehlwani style who remained undefeated throughout his career. His physical condition was so exceptional that he achieved legendary status. In the Indian subcontinent, he became an icon of resistance against European colonialism. Bruce Lee was an avid follower of Gama's training routine. Having read about the exercises that helped Gama develop his legendary strength as a wrestler, Bruce incorporated some of these methods into his own routines.

I then went back to England in order to wrestle a match with the renowned veteran, Tom Cannon, This took place on September 27, 1902, at Liverpool, and lasted thirty-three minutes. The English champion, though now somewhat of a veteran, had had a very wide and exceptional experience, and was able to bring into play some very skilful, if somewhat painful, moves, which he had picked up from Turkish wrestlers. I managed, however, to secure a hammerlock and Cannon succumbed.

Not satisfied with this result, Cannon, after staying out a fifteen-minute "limit" contest, made another match "to a finish" with me, which I won fairly easily.

This success, though not a very arduous one for me, was generally regarded as a great feather in my cap, and I received a number of excellent engagements to wrestle in England and Scotland in consequence.

I entered my name for the Gold Belt contest in Paris (November, 1902), but they sought to impose a number of peddling counter proposals, to which I could not see my way to consent, a result which seemed to be highly acceptable to the Paris authorities, as it was apparently intended that the favourite, Pons, whom I had already thrice defeated, should win. I did not regret this, as Pons is a first-rate man.

After this, I toured all over England, being successful against every wrestler who accepted my challenge to all comers.

In 1903, I met and defeated the following wrestlers: Tom Cannon, Tom Connors, Tom MacInerney, and Tom Clayton. I threw all of them but was unfortunately laid up with an attack of rheumatism brought on by the damp climate of Glasgow, which prevented my taking part in the contest for the Championship of the World in Paris. In this contest, Pedersen was first and Raoul de Boucher second, both of whom I had previously defeated.

Owing to the fact that the "Catch-as-catch-can" style of wrestling is the more usual and favourite method in England, I was frequently obliged to wrestle with my opponents in this method, but, thanks to my strength and presence of mind, I always came off the conqueror. I very often trained specially for this style with Jack Smith of Manchester, a very clever wrestler.

In September, 1903, I wrestled with Bech Olsen, who had, however, no claims to be considered a first-class wrestler. The contest, however, came to an unsatisfactory termination, as, owing to an accident to my ankle, the match had to be discontinued.

On the strength of this, Antonio Pieri, "the terrible Greek," challenged me to wrestle with him, hoping that I would fall an easy victim. The match came off about the middle of October at the Oxford Music Hall, in London, and I threw this very experienced and—in spite of his years—very dangerous adversary, in twenty-five minutes. Pieri challenged me to a return match to be decided by one fall under Greco-Roman, and one under "Catch-as-catch-can" rules. We met on November 21, and in the first bout (Greco-Roman) I beat him in 17 min. 11 sec. by means of a "half-nelson," and in the second bout, which followed immediately after, in "Catch-as-catch-can" style, I threw him in 15 min. 25 sec.

Smarting under his defeat, Pieri set himself to work to unearth a wrestler who could beat me. And before very long he introduced to the British public a Turk named Ahmed Madrali, a man of gigantic strength, who was boomed in every possible manner as being a better man than myself. At first, I paid but little attention to these attacks, as I had a great many excellent engagements in London and in many other large English towns, where I defeated everyone who came into the ring against me. At last, however, I took up his challenge, and we met on January 30, 1904, at Olympia in London, with the winning of two falls out of three to decide the match. The Turk was 6 ft. I in. in height and weighed 16 st. A huge audience had assembled when the Turk entered the ring with Antonio Pieri, whilst I was accompanied by Koch. The contest, as will be remembered, was a very brief one, as on Madrali making a move for my waist, I dashed in, lifted him off his feet, and threw him onto his shoulders. Unfortunately, he fell on his arm, and as this was dislocated, he was unable to continue the contest, but luckily was able to begin wrestling again three months later.

This victory raised my reputation to its zenith, and since that time, I don't think I had a wrestling rival in the affections or esteem of the British public.

There is no need for me to enter into any description of the troubles, legal and otherwise, connected with my next big encounter. They were far from being pleasant to either Jenkins or myself, but since neither of us wished to disappoint the public, we readily agreed to the final makeshift arrangements and met on the mat before 6,000 people at the Albert Hall on July 2, 1904. I early on succeeded in getting "behind" the American champion, but after a five minutes' struggle, he succeeded in breaking loose. Three times afterwards, I threw him on the mat, but he managed to wriggle out of a fall. Jenkins struggled hard and displayed very good defensive tactics, but was forced finally to succumb to a "half-nelson" after 20 min. 37 sec. of wrestling. After a fifteen-minute interval, Jenkins opened the second bout with an aggressive movement, and for some little time, we had a stand-up struggle. Again, we went to the mat, where, in spite of his utmost efforts, I finally managed to pin him out after 14 min. 27 sec. The Sportsman report of this match read as follows:

"It was ten o'clock before the rivals appeared on the platform. By this time, the spectators were in a high state of enthusiasm and gave the men a ringing cheer. Taking stock of the two men, it was clear that Hackenschmidt had the advantage, physically speaking, at every turn. He looked a stone and a half heavier, deeper and more solid about the chest, more firmly set on the limbs, and had nearly twice the muscular development of the American. Jenkins is a strongly-built man, but he did not appear half so fit as his opponent, carrying too much flesh. For all that, he made a creditable show and gave one the impression of being a man of real grit, resource, and stamina.

"When the men got to grips, Hackenschmidt attacked in decisive style, and twice just missed with the flying mare. In less than three minutes, he fixed his

DIFFERENCES BETWEEN CATCH AND GRECO-ROMAN WRESTLING

The basic differences between Greco-Roman Wrestling (attacks above the waist, aiming to throw the opponent so that their back touches the ground) and Catch-As-Catch-Can (a full-fledged wrestling style that even allows holds on the feet and limbs) are clear. Often, specialists in one style would not want to compete under the rules of the other.

The foundations of Catch wrestling come from ancient folk styles and Greco-Roman wrestling itself. A Catch competition could be decided by the best of three falls or by submission (where the opponent quits due to a hold, submission, or exhaustion). The majority of submission techniques were used to either make the opponent fall or keep them in a submissive position with their back on the ground.

At that time, the concept of joint locks or strangulation techniques, which are more modern and used in Brazilian Jiu-Jitsu and contemporary submission wrestling, did not exist.

Hackenschmidt had to learn to master all these styles. He had a record of 300 wins in Greco-Roman wrestling (and over 2,000 wins in total) and is considered by some to be the second greatest wrestler of all time. For example, the title of World Heavyweight Champion was created in 1905 when he defeated the American Tom Jenkins. Additionally, Hackenschmidt won the European Heavyweight Greco-Roman Championship and received several posthumous awards: Professional Wrestling Hall of Fame and Museum, Wrestling Observer Newsletter, and WWE Hall of Fame in 2016.

rival in a cruel body grip and swung him over onto the stage. Jenkins endeavoured to spring forward onto his feet, but Hackenschmidt's arms shot out like lightning, and he pulled his man down with the greatest ease. The American defended very cleverly, and, failing to find an opening for an arm-hold, the Russian picked his opponent up with the intention of pitching him over his back. Jenkins smartly eluded his grip, and after six minutes, both were on their feet. Hackenschmidt was forcing the pace at a terrific rate, and three times lifted his man up and brought him to the boards with a magnificent display of strength, but it availed nothing against the American's skilful defence. Again, Hackenschmidt attempted the flying mare, but his hand slipped on his opponent's neck, and like a flash, Jenkins gripped the Russian by the waist and had him down. The wrestling was now more even, and each man attacked in turn. The strength and science which the challenger exhibited were a complete revelation, and he kept his opponent at bay without much difficulty. When a quarter of an hour had gone, Hackenschmidt rushed in and swung Jenkins bodily round the stage, describing three circles before he threw him to the boards, but the American once more eluded his grip like an eel. Then the Russian braced himself for a big effort. Twice he twisted Jenkins over onto one shoulder, and just as promptly did Jenkins, with a mighty contraction of his neck and shoulder muscles, snap the holds. At this point, Jenkins mysteriously weakened. Hackenschmidt bore down on him with the power of a Hercules, and with a pedal action similar to a man pushing a heavy roller up a hill, forced his man over on his back, and with an irresistible 'half-nelson' gained the first fall in 20 min. 37 sec."

"In the second bout, Hackenschmidt did most of the attacking, but Jenkins again put up a wonderfully plucky and skilful defence. Once the latter forgot himself and the rules by employing the leg-hold, but Hackenschmidt appeared quite unruffled by an act which ought to have been penalized by disqualification. Minute after minute sped by, but Jenkins could put on nothing more dangerous than a back-of-the-neck hold in answer to the Russian's arm-hold. Then Hackenschmidt brought the 'half-nelson' into play, but when Jenkins seemed in hopeless plight, he extricated himself by a magnificent feat of wrestling, a subtlety that evoked a tremendous storm of cheering. It proved his last expiring effort, however, for before he had quite recovered from the exhaustion which the struggle had engendered, the Russian had cleverly slipped on a second 'half-nelson,' and Jenkins was placed squarely on his shoulders in 14 min. 27 sec. Jenkins is to be congratulated on his plucky fight and his fine display of wrestling. The cheer which he received after his defeat was quite as hearty as that accorded Hackenschmidt."

Leaving England in September, 1904, I set out for a four-month tour in the Antipodes. My first experiences in Australia were unfortunately by no means as pleasant as they might have been, for I had to go into the hospital very soon after my arrival in Sydney. I was not able to fulfil any of my engagements for quite five weeks, owing to both my arm and my knee again giving way. I was suffering from what are commonly called a housemaid's knee and a miner's elbow, which means water on both joints, necessitating an operation.

This was successful, and I was able to get to work, touring through all the principal towns and meeting all the wrestlers of note whom I could come across. Prior to my arrival in the Southern Continent, the two wrestlers who had enjoyed the biggest reputations were two big Hindus, Buttan Singh and Gunga Brahm. Both of these were fine big men, with plenty of strength and considerable skill, yet I threw the pair of them in nine minutes on the same night.

Clarence Weber, however, the Champion All-round Athlete of Australia, a most splendidly built young fellow, managed to hold out for ten minutes on more than one occasion. I may say, though, that I did not make any special preparation for either of these encounters, and owing, of course, to my having to wrestle different opponents nearly every night, I was naturally a bit weary and lacking in fire and vigour.

As Greco-Roman wrestling was not well understood in Australia, I found it occasionally difficult to fix up matters with the various opponents who presented themselves and was consequently compelled to devote my attention seriously to the study of the "Catch-as-catch-can" style. This was an important stage in my career, and, considering that I was practically staking all my hard-earned reputation on my prospects of success under these new and comparatively strange rules, a somewhat risky step to contemplate. Nevertheless, I accepted the situation, and can sincerely acknowledge that I have never regretted having done so.

After a fairly considerable experience, I may now confess that I distinctly preferred the more open method, and did not again propose deserting "catch-as-catch-can". I did indeed make publicly a declaration of my determination never to wrestle under Greco-Roman rules again.

By the way, on one occasion while in Australia, I was challenged to wrestle in the Cornish style of wrestling, in which a fall is secured only when a wrestler is thrown on any three points, viz., both shoulders and one hip, or both hips and a shoulder touch the ground. All bouts are contested from a standing position, and a hold is secured on the jacket which each contestant has to wear.

My challenger, Delhi Nielsen, who was an experienced Cornish wrestler, may perhaps have imagined that at this style (to which I was quite unaccustomed) he might very probably enjoy a comparatively even chance with me. Having defeated over 400 opponents and possessing an untarnished record, he was, in fact, very confident.

He consequently refused to wrestle with me, save under these conditions, and I was compelled to agree to his terms, trusting that my acquaintance with the Russian style of wrestling, with waist-belts (between which and the Cornish style there is a very faint resemblance, although tripping is prohibited under the Russian rules), might stand me in good stead.

Be that as it may, I was able to rise to the occasion and to throw him very easily.

Having completed my Australian engagements, during the course of which I defeated Grotz, who was called the Champion of South Africa, and several other prominent wrestlers and physical culturists, I paid a brief visit to New Zealand, and then sailed for America, where I was booked for several engagements, the most important of all being my return match with Tom Jenkins, the American champion, whom I had defeated under Greco-Roman rules at the Albert Hall on July 2, 1904.

On my way across the Pacific, I made a brief stay at the island of Samoa, and can well understand the enthusiasm with which travelers in the South Seas always refer to those havens of bliss, the islands of Polynesia.

I had promised to meet Jenkins in this return encounter in New York, after the London contest, and now agreed that our second meeting should be under "Catch-as-catch-can" rules, with which my opponent was more familiar, but at which style I had but little experience, save for an occasional encounter in England and more frequently during my Australian tour. This match with Jenkins, however, was the first big one in which I had engaged entirely under "Catch-as-catch-can" rules, and considerable interest was, perhaps, naturally felt throughout America on this account.

Jenkins and I met before a huge crowd at the Madison Square Gardens, New York, on May 4, 1905, our respective weights being as follows: Jenkins 14 st. 4 Ib. and my own 14 st. 12 Ib.

I was not yet sufficiently versed in the style at which we were wrestling to forestall the clever leg-locks and holds by which my opponent contrived to postpone disaster. He was mostly on the defensive, wriggling and extricating himself from difficulties in a very able manner, but despite a very strenuous struggle and a determined bridge, I finally managed to lever him over and pin him down in 31 min. 14 sec.

He seemed very exhausted, but recovered well, and exhibited considerable liveliness when we met for the second bout. He secured a "half-nelson" and a crotch-hold, and several times initiated an attack, but I did not experience much difficulty in breaking clear from the holds he managed to secure. I gradually wore him down, and, finally fixing a "half-nelson," forced him over despite his struggles, pinning him down for the second time in 22 min. 4 sec. A typical American report of this match ran as follows:

"New York, May 5.—Geo. Hackenschmidt, the Russian Lion, defeated Tom Jenkins, the American champion wrestler, in two straight falls last night at Madison Square Gardens, in a match in which Jenkins was handled like a pigmy

KARA AHMED

Razgard, Ottoman Empire (Bulgaria) [1870-1902]

He was a famous Bulgarian-born wrestler who was part of the so-called "Turkish Invasion" in the world of wrestling. He became the World Heavyweight Wrestling Champion in the second edition of the tournament in Paris (1899).
Repeatedly mentioned in this book, Hack recognized him as an excellent wrestler.
He continued his professional wrestling career in Germany for several years but tragically died at the age of 32.

in the hands of a giant. Hackenschmidt broke holds as if they were the clutchings of a child.

"For half an hour the Russian Lion battered Jenkins without a moment's cessation. The older man's vitality began to ebb. Suddenly Hackenschmidt got a 'half-nelson' lock on him—both hands up under the chest and clasped around his neck. Inch by inch he twisted Jenkins over, still over, till both shoulders touched the mat. But Referee Hurst did not see the fall and signalled to go on. Within a minute Hackenschmidt repeated the feat, and this time he kept his man bored down until Hurst dragged him off. Time, 31 min. 15 sec.

"Tom was still tired when he came back fifteen minutes later for the second bout. Patiently, bravely, unflinchingly, almost hopefully, he put forth all his cunning and strength. Once, as they stood face to face, Hackenschmidt seized Jenkins under the arms and whirled him around in a furious waltz. The body of Jenkins stood out straight, his feet pointing at the horizontal. Twice thus around he went; then Hackenschmidt slammed him down on the floor. Tom wriggled around so that his shoulders did not touch the mat. It was a wonderful exhibition of quick thinking under adverse circumstances. But Tom's bolt was shot. No mere human giant could last under the awful strain of handling Hackenschmidt. After 22 min. and 4 sec. the Russian again put Jenkins down with a 'half-nelson.' Poor old Tom was hardly able to walk out of the ring. Hackenschmidt dashed away as briskly as ever."

"I would like to have thrown him quicker," he said, "but several times when I had good holds on him he turned very white and I was afraid of hurting him, so I let up."

Despite the strenuous nature of this match, I felt very little fatigue or exhaustion afterwards, thanks to my excellent condition. I was able to demonstrate this on the following evening, when I was matched to throw half-a-dozen wrestlers of considerable local prominence under Graeco-Roman rules. This was a fairly stiff contract, but I managed to dispose of the whole half-dozen inside eighteen minutes.

James Parr, the old Lancashire wrestler, then challenged me to throw him the next evening, offering to resist being thrown three times within the hour. He was, of course, giving a fair amount of weight, but as he is a very skilful wrestler I consider that I did not do at all badly by pinning him down three times in 7 min. 50 sec.

During my tour in the States I had a rather amusing experience in St. Louis. I was there matched against Jean Baptiste, who was the champion wrestler of the district.

As soon as the match was arranged I was attacked by malarial fever, and, consulting a doctor, was ordered to bed, where I speedily became much worse, my temperature rising as high as 105 degrees.

FRANK GOTCH

Iowa, United States [1877-1917]

He was an American professional wrestler and the first to claim the title of World Heavyweight Wrestling Champion, which he held for five years (from 1908 to 1913). He played a pivotal role in popularizing wrestling in the United States and can be considered one of the country's most famous athletes during the first decade of the 20th century.

Throughout his career, he defeated notable wrestlers such as Tom Jenkins, Ben Roller, Stanislaus Zbyszko, Georg Lurich, and the legendary George Hackenschmidt.

Gotch was undoubtedly an excellent wrestler, known for both his technique and strategy. However, without diminishing his impressive career, his contemporaries agree that his most pronounced trait was being known as "a dirty wrestler".

Under these circumstances, and especially as the doctor considered my condition to be highly critical, I sent to the match promoters and informed them that it would be impossible for me to fulfil my engagement on the date agreed.

They called to see me in a state of great distress, represented that their outlay had been considerable, that they had sold a large number of tickets, and that if they were forced to return the money they had received for these they would be completely ruined.

They implored me to meet Baptiste and used so many arguments that I was practically compelled to assent, provided I found myself able to leave my bed, and although I was still very ill on the day of the match I managed to struggle down to the scene of our encounter.

Arrived there with the doctor by my side, I felt so weak, ill and giddy, that I could not summon up sufficient energy to change my attire, and was sitting shivering and shaking with fever, when I overheard my opponent in the next dressing-room asserting that he would not meet me, as I should be sure to kill him. The promoters were busy trying to encourage him, and as a last resource brought him into my dressing-room that I might assure him that I would be gentle and would handle him tenderly.

I was able to do this confidently, as at the moment I felt scarcely strong enough to wrestle with a child.

However, the humour of the situation so appealed to me that I had difficulty in restraining my laughter, and after Baptiste, now somewhat more courageous, had retired to get ready I was able to undress and to get into my wrestling trunks.

I felt somewhat better, but was still so weak that I positively reeled as I mounted the steps to the raised platform on which we were to wrestle, and experienced considerable difficulty in getting through the ropes which surrounded the mat.

Once there, my strength seemed to come back to me, and the sight of my timid adversary nerved me to go through the ordeal.

In his state of nervousness and terror, he was, perhaps, not a very formidable opponent, but he was, nevertheless, very big and strong and but for the nervous strength with which I have been endowed and which seemed to suddenly come back to me in full tide, I might have had a stiff bargain.

However, as matters went, I did not experience much trouble, throwing him three times in fairly quick time, and subsequently a Turk, Ali Muralah by name. This last opponent was styled "the terrible Turk," but I have never heard of him before that day, nor have I heard of him since. After which I returned to bed and to my doctor's care and indignation. He was very wroth and told me that I had practically done my best to commit suicide, but my constitution pulled me through, and I have since experienced no ill effects from my adventure.

After finishing my engagements in the States I paid a visit to Canada, where I threw such opponents as I could meet with. The most formidable of these was the celebrated French-Canadian, Emile Maupas, a strong and clever wrestler. He was an adept at the reversed body hold, which he tried on with me, but barely succeeded in lifting me from the mat, then losing his balance and falling backwards. I threw him three times in less than twenty-one and a half minutes, the first fall occupying 7 min. 39 sec., the second 6 min, 19 sec., and the third 7 min. 20 sec.

After visiting the Falls of Niagara, and doing a little sightseeing, I again set sail for England, where I was booked to appear for a week in Manchester, before appearing at the Canterbury Music Hall on Whit-Monday. Back again in the British Isles with a long list of music-hall engagements before me and having anticipations of a prospective match with Alexander Munro (the Scottish champion) and a possible return encounter with Madrali, it was quite clear that on these occasions my opponents would stipulate for "Catch-as-catch-can" conditions, and that it would be advisable for me to accustom myself thoroughly to that style of wrestling.

I therefore resolved that, at all events for the time being, I would only engage in contests or exhibitions under that code, more especially as there can be

IVAN PODDUBNY

Born in 1871 in Krasenivka, part of the Russian Empire, now Ukraine. At the age of 20, he was forced to leave his home to work as a stevedore in the ports of Sevastopol and Feodosiya. It was there that Ivan began training with kettlebells and participating in amateur wrestling.
By 1905, he had become the World Wrestling Champion in Paris.
During the 1920s, Ivan traveled to the United States in search of new challenges and had a highly successful tour where he remained undefeated.
Throughout his life, he maintained a professional rivalry with the famous Polish wrestler Stanislaus Zbyszko. During the Nazi occupation of Russia, Ivan rejected the offer to leave the Soviet Union to train German wrestlers.

no doubt of its greater popularity among the British people. Several months elapsed before the conditions could be arranged for my encounter with Munro, and meanwhile I had my music-hall engagements to fulfil, but finally, on October 28, 1905, I encountered the British champion before 16,000 spectators on the Glasgow Rangers' Football Ground, at Ibrox Park. The greatest interest was evinced in the encounter on account of my antagonist's magnificent physique and great reputation. My readers may, perhaps, be interested in comparing our respective weights and measurements on that occasion:

MUNRO	HACKENSCHMIDT
Height: 6 ft.	5 ft, 9¼ in
Weight: 15 st. 5 lb.	14 st. 8 lb.
Neck: 18 in.	22 in.
Chest: 48 in.	52 in.
Waist: 36 in.	34 in.
Thigh: 27 in.	26¼ in.
Calf: 17 in.	18 in.
Forearm: 14¾ in.	15¼ in.
Biceps: 17¼ in.	19 in.

A drizzling rain which fell throughout the contest somewhat hampered my movements, and since I was the attacking party during most of the time the conditions naturally handicapped me more seriously than my adversary. Munro was the first to go to the mat, and was soon compelled to "bridge" for safety. I turned him over with a leg hold, but he managed to slip clear, as he also did out of several "half-nelsons." Indeed, after about a quarter of an hour's struggle he managed so to extricate himself from my grasp as to be able to put in several aggressive movements. He was, and is undoubtedly, a very powerful man, and did not finally succumb (to a "half-nelson") until after a struggle lasting altogether 22 min. 40 sec.

After ten minutes' interval we commenced the second bout and again the Scotchman displayed fine defensive tactics, once or twice even assuming the offensive. Again, however, I got him with a "half-nelson" and rolled him over in 11 min. 11 sec.

That night, on appearing to fulfil my engagement at the Palace Theatre, just outside Glasgow, the audience called for a speech, and after my saying a few words they stood up as one man and gave me one of the biggest ovations I had ever experienced in Great Britain. The kindly enthusiasm with which they acclaimed me as "a jolly good fellow" was such as I shall never forget, for the rest of my life. My music-hall engagements, together with an occasional brief holiday, occupied me now for the next six months, when, in order to satisfy Madrali, Pieri, the British public and myself that the result of our first encounter was not, as Pieri alleged, "a fluke," I consented to again meet the "Terrible Turk" under "Catch-as-catch-can" rules on this occasion. At this style of wrestling, he was, according to his mentor and discoverer, "absolutely invincible," and on the strength of recent encounters with Tom Jenkins and Alex Munro, a not inconsiderable section of the public inclined to the opinion that he would "make me travel." Even I myself had but little confidence in my chance, consequently I trained seriously for the occasion, putting in a fortnight's preparation at dear old Jack Grumley's house, 'The Seven Stars,' Shepherd's Bush. I had practice bouts regularly with one or other of the following very capable group of wrestlers: Jack Smith, "Gunner" Moir, poor Jack Grumley, John Strong, Gus Rennart, and Constables Barrett and Humphreys of the City Police, and to wind up, I took them all to Worthing and finished my training there. One daily item of my training may deserve mention here, since in itself it was no small feat and, graduated according to circumstances, might be included with advantage in every wrestler's preparation. I used to kneel down while the others placed a sack of cement weighing six hundred-weight on my back, and as soon as this was comfortably settled, poor Jack Grumley, who scaled another 232 lbs., seated himself thereon, say, well, over 900 lbs. in all. No small weight-moving feat I can assure you. Under these circumstances, therefore, it can be well understood that I was feeling particularly fit and well when for the second occasion I faced Madrali at Olympia. As this contest was brought about after a tremendously wordy discussion in the Press and amidst the greatest possible excitement, it may, perhaps, interest my readers if I quote the report which appeared in The Manchester Guardian and ran as follows:

"Hackenschmidt and Madrali, surrounded by their friends and seconds, were early in their dressing-rooms. Madrali was reported marvellously fit but a whisper flew round, among the journalists, telling the alarming tale that Hackenschmidt was sick! His stomach was wrong! They were anointing him with alcohol! He was faint! He was trembling. Part of it was true. Sheer excitement had upset the Russian, and betting began to veer, and the odds weakened just as they do on the morning of a big race, when the favourite is reported to be coughing. Strung to a higher pitch of excitement by this 'stable intelligence,' the crowd watched and waited hungrily for the appearance of the two mighty men. It was nearly half-past nine before the band played with great gusto, 'See the conquering hero comes!' There was a sudden eddy

NECESSARY VILLAINS?

It seems almost necessary to create antagonistic figures in books, stories, and even life itself. In the history of Saxon, we already find the antagonistic and almost demonized figure of Sandow. In this book, it seems that the almost villainous (or weak and cowardly) figures are Lurich and Gotch. So, the big question that the impartial reader faces is: were they truly the villains as portrayed? Or were they scapegoats, much like the albino monk Bai Mei in the story of the destruction of the Shaolin temple, or Goldstein as the figure of hatred (metaphorically representing Trotsky) in George Orwell's 1984?

By 1900, wrestling had become a massive spectacle with significant commercial interests. It was almost necessary to create or invent rivalries to satisfy the public's desires, much like modern television does today.

among the group of privileged persons at the side of the ring, the eddy broke and through it strode Madrali. Olympia howled as one man. The Turk stalked on to the stage like a ghost in a dream. He looked immense—passionless and colourless; a black overcoat covered him from throat to ankles."

He walked to his corner like an automaton and sat down stiffly on a kitchen chair. At the tail end of the cheers which greeted him came Hackenschmidt, in a brown dressing-gown, with tassels flapping dolorously. With his wonderful shoulders concealed by the wrappings of his gown, he appeared small and puny compared with the great mass of humanity opposite him. His face—frank and boyish as a rule—was the very picture of misery. It was drab and drawn and withered. His lips were trembling and his eyes were flashing furtive glances across the great auditorium, whilst the cheers hurtled among the rafters of the glass dome...

"At the call of 'time,' and in a silence through which one little cough broke like a rifle shot, the Turk and the Russian leaped like cats to the mat. And at that moment life and confidence came back to Hackenschmidt, whose apparent collapse was nothing more than tremendous excitement worked up to a pitch almost heartbreaking. He knew that in the 'Catch-as-catch-can' style Madrali was cunning and relentless if he could only get time—time to wear his man down and to grind the spirit out of him. And Hackenschmidt's one idea was to limit the time to a mere handful of seconds, if he only could, and not save himself for an endurance test. After a few lightning flashes of preliminary sparring, the Russian jumped in for a neck hold and got Madrali's head down. But Madrali weaved his arms round Hackenschmidt's waist and hugged and tugged until his opponent bent nearly double. Hackenschmidt made a wild grab at the Turk's neck and got a hold which was near enough to the 'strangle grip' to cause Madrali to squirm away and protest, mumbling to the referee as he explained in pantomimic passes with his hands. In another moment, the pair were at it again, crouching like tigers for a spring. And here Madrali made his first bad mistake. He tried his favourite dodge—a sudden spring to get a leg hold. But Hackenschmidt, sharp as a needle, was on the look-out for that. He hopped back an inch and no more, Madrali's hand smote the air and the impetus of his fruitless

GAMA VS ZBYSZKO

When the Great Gama arrived in London, he announced a public challenge to "Any European wrestler of any weight category who dares to face him for 30 minutes." Initially, the European wrestling world saw it as a sensationalist announcement, and no one accepted the challenge. So, Gama raised the stakes and explicitly challenged the champions of Europe and the United States, Stanislaus Zbyszko and Frank Gotch, respectively. "If I do not defeat them, I will personally pay the prize money and return home".

The first professional wrestler to accept the challenge was the American Benjamin Roller. Gama defeated him in 1 minute and 40 seconds in the first match and in 9 minutes and 10 seconds in the second.

The following day, he defeated 12 European professional wrestlers consecutively, thus gaining access to the official tournaments. The event made headlines in the world of international wrestling. This caught the attention of Zbyszko, who accepted the challenge.

The match took place on September 10, 1910. The contest lasted a total of 2 and a half hours, after which it was declared a draw. The match was rescheduled for the following week, September 17. However, Stanislaus Zbyszko never showed up, and Gama was declared the winner.

Seventeen years later, Zbyszko challenged Gama to a rematch, this time in India. The contest lasted only 40 seconds, and Gama was victorious once again. It is worth noting that Zbyszko was at the end of his career, attempting to regain his fortune, which he had nearly lost completely during World War I. There are rumors that the fight was "fixed" between Zbyszko and the Maharaja of Patiala, who sponsored the event, for a large sum of money.

It is also important to note that Gama's trips abroad were sponsored by the Maharaja of Datia, with the intention of showcasing the power of the Indian subcontinent as a protest against European colonialism. While this made Gama a hero in his homeland, it hindered his opportunities as a professional wrestler elsewhere in the world.

ZBYSZKO

grab upset his balance. His right arm went up to steady himself, and like an arrow, the Russian leaped in, took his man under that right arm, and swung him round. Down with a thud and a grunt went the Turk. Hackenschmidt was on him, and Madrali went over in a body-roll, which no power on earth could stop. There was one wild struggle, a helpless kick or two, and Madrali was pinned to the carpet in a fair and straight throw in 1 min. 34 sec. Madrali staggered up, shook himself, and stalked back to his corner, while in a storm of cheers, Hackenschmidt, pale as death but smiling, slipped on his dressing-gown and departed to his dressing-room for the fifteen minutes' interval. Madrali stayed where he was, solacing himself with a rough towel.

"For the second bout, the Russian was a raging favourite. And lo! in the second bout, Madrali found his haven. Twice he dived for the leg hold. Twice he got it, being craftier this time, after his first stinging lesson in carelessness. Twice Hackenschmidt broke away. And then, in a whirl of heaving flesh, both men came to earth with a bump. Madrali was on top. He wriggled behind the Russian and wrapped his sinewy arms round his waist. Hackenschmidt crouched on all fours, while Madrali kneaded him remorselessly—a painful process which has churned many a great wrestler into sickness and partial unconsciousness. A minute or so of this set the Russian sweating. His white skin glistened in the blaze of the electric light. His face was twisted with pain. And still, the inexorable Turk gruelled and gruelled his opponent. Thinking, no doubt, he had weakened him sufficiently, he made a grab at his ankle. That did not come off, so Madrali ground his knee into the Russian's thigh. This was not strictly cricket, and Mr. Dunning promptly stopped it. Hackenschmidt just watched for his chance. It came with startling suddenness. Incautiously, Madrali loosed his waist hold and tried a 'half-nelson' on the Russian's right arm, but found it too strong even for his muscles, whereupon Hackenschmidt got a left wrist hold and a leg-lock simultaneously, strained the mighty muscles of his shoulders almost to bursting-point, and with a heave which showed incredible strength, hurled his man clean over. The crowd went mad with excitement. 'He's got him! He's got him!' they yelled. He had. Fiercely, furiously, panting and straining,

Hackenschmidt flung his whole weight upon the prostrate Turk. It was the biggest effort he had ever made. For a breathless moment, Madrali struggled. Then he collapsed with a sob, and Mr. Dunning smote Hackenschmidt upon the shoulders with a sounding slap which signalized that the championship had been won and that the terrible Turk had been beaten. 'Time, four minutes,' cried Mr. Mansell, the timekeeper, and like an avalanche, the crowd swarmed, roaring into the arena."

Since that date, it has become fashionable in certain quarters to call Madrali a much overrated man. There never was a worse, or indeed a more absurd, mistake. He was a most formidable opponent, one of the strongest, if not actually the strongest, man I have ever encountered. Somewhat careless, perhaps, as a wrestler, but once he had you in his clutches—well, he had me pretty tightly, I admit, and I was able to turn the tables, but I shall always count myself as singularly fortunate in having been able to do so. Tom Jenkins is a very powerful man and a most able wrestler, and yet Madrali positively crushed him. Munro is one of the strongest men in the world, and thoroughly experienced at "Catch-as-catch-can," and yet Madrali treated him almost as if he were a novice. No, the opinions which were entertained of the "Terrible Turk" prior to his defeat by me were much nearer the truth than those which obtained subsequently thereto, and every wrestler who ever felt Madrali's grip will, I am sure, fully endorse this opinion.

I was now booked up for a lengthy tour, during which I visited nearly every town in the United Kingdom, meeting all the wrestlers of repute in every locality, without coming across any serious or exciting encounter.

In August 1907, my old knee trouble again made its appearance, but this time the water gathered in the joint itself, so that my knee cap stood away from the joint quite a quarter of an inch. By medical advice, I now always wore a bandage and found it practically impossible to do any serious wrestling practice. Even a slow trot caused me such pain that I could only fulfil my ordinary engagements with the utmost difficulty.

Matters in the wrestling world were livened up, however, by the visit of three wrestlers possessing formidable reputations on the Continent.

First came Constant le Marin, then the Galician wrestler, Cyganiewicz, or Zbysco. Finally came the big Cossack, Padoubny, the winner of World's Championship Tournaments in the Greco-Roman style.

These were followed by Joe Rogers, a big American wrestler, with whom I had wrestled in New York, but who had since progressed considerably in his knowledge of the game.

All four of these hurled challenges at me, but as I found that Constant le Marin, who had been first in the field, appeared less ready to come to business than he had been to announce his readiness therefor, and as it would have been absurd to match myself to meet them all at once or to lay myself open to their accusations if I accorded either of them precedence, I suggested that they had better wrestle among themselves, promising to meet the winner.

Knowing full well that they were all formidable opponents, and feeling the urgent need of rest and recuperation after my long and arduous spell of work, I now took a brief holiday, paying a visit to my home in Russia.

Unfortunately, I did not find the rest or cure I needed, and consequently, returned to England feeling far from fit and well, in time to witness the Zbysco-Padoubny match, to which the proposed tournament had dwindled down.

This, as may be remembered, resulted in the victory of Zbysco, owing to the disqualification of Padoubny, and I accordingly signed articles to meet the winner.

Meanwhile, Rogers, who had been unable to enter the proposed tournament or triangular contest, owing to a poisoned thumb, was clamouring for a match with me, on the plea that I had promised to meet him while I was in America, if he took up wrestling seriously and was able to prove that he was a serious opponent.

HACK VS. GOTCH

This he had done by virtue of his success in one or two American tournaments in which he had defeated some very formidable opponents, and so I consented to meet him.

We came together at the Oxford Music Hall on February 6, 1908, and, despite his great advantage in height and weight (he was quite six inches taller and more than three stone heavier than I was), I did not experience any very great difficulty in pinning him out twice in 7 min. 35 sec. and 6 min. 45 sec. respectively. I was attacking practically throughout the contest, almost the only aggressive move he made being an attempt to seize me around the thighs, which resulted in his being thrown for the first time,

THE TRUE WAY OF LIVING?

In interviews and other books, Hack engages in an interesting self-analysis of his work. He asserts that the "way of living" is different for each person. Having clarified in this book that his intention is not only to establish rules for strong men and women, but also to strengthen the health and strength of the average person, he still allows himself to question his own thoughts. He wonders if each individual and the variations present in each person would make the way of living something unique and special, changing from person to person.

I believe that this model of thinking is not self-criticism, but rather a legitimate question about the variabilities and "it depends" for each being. This open and relative way of thinking, which takes into account the constitutive, biopsychosocial variables that can arise in each individual, makes his work not only ahead of its time but also unique in the conceptual and editorial world of physical culture. This, one of his earliest books, is direct, raw, practical, and real. However, within it, we already see this unstructured thought emerging, which later would project itself into works written decades later, where Hackenschmidt begins to move away from the "earthly" plane of strength and structure to ask philosophical and even existential questions, possibly completing the communion so often mentioned by the Chinese, between the earth, man, and heaven.

as I stooped also and quicker than he did, securing a hold just below his knees, lifting him, and then pitching him forcibly to the ground, after which I was able to pin him down without much difficulty. I then sailed to America to fulfil my contract to wrestle Frank Gotch. Prior to the contest itself, I fulfilled a night's engagement at the Grand Central Palace, New York, meeting Neil Olsen, a quick little wrestler who called himself Young Hackenschmidt, and Steg-Miller, whom I took with me to America. After this, I went to Boston, where I wrestled John Perelli, Albert Ouvray, and several others; and had the honor of making the acquaintance of the son of President Roosevelt, who introduced me to his friends. From Boston, I went to Philadelphia, and there beat Carl Darschen of Camden, in 33 min., Henry Paulson in 5 min. 9 sec., and Miller. From Philadelphia, I went to Washington, where I was introduced to President Roosevelt at the White House, and to several other leading politicians. There I wrestled five opponents, and threw them all pretty quickly; traveling thence to Baltimore, where, after defeating two or three opponents, I wrestled 15 min. with Gus Schénlein (America). From here I went straight to Chicago to get ready for Gotch. As to the contest itself, so much has been said and written already by various eyewitnesses and also by people who were not eyewitnesses, that it seems to me that I should be serving no useful purpose by either adding to or taking from the remarks I have already made on the subject. After returning to England, I had to prepare for a match with Zbysco, which should have taken place in June. I started hard practice, but in a short time, felt such pain in my right knee, around the kneecap, that it was even painful to walk. Any quick turn made me feel as though I should collapse. I cancelled all my engagements, including the match, and went to Aix-la-Cha-pelle to undergo a thorough treatment. When did I last hold a championship?

ГЕОРГ   О.ЛАНГСЕПГ
ГАККЕНШМИДТ

When I entered for and won the Championship Tournaments in Vienna, Berlin, and Paris in the year 1901, the motive that actuated me was the desire to prove myself a greater wrestler than all the famous exponents of the science who were gathered together at those places. That I won the title of champion at the same time was purely a side issue. So much so, indeed, that I have not since troubled about renewing it.

Throughout my whole career, I have never bothered as to whether I was a champion or not a champion. The only title I have desired to be known by is simply my name, George Hackenschmidt.

EPILOGUE

I never imagined that in the translation and compilation of this work, I would learn so much. The concepts and ideas in this manual remain more relevant than ever and inspire us to elevate ourselves not only as practitioners but also as whole and evolved humans. Few words remain that can add anything to this epic re-edition that has just been completed. Hackenschmidt's legacy in the history of strength and wrestling is truly decisive. Hack is perhaps one of the few and most important figures in the pursuit of communion between strength, wrestling, and living in health and harmony. Embarking on this task has changed something in me forever. I hope it has had some effect on your way of living too!

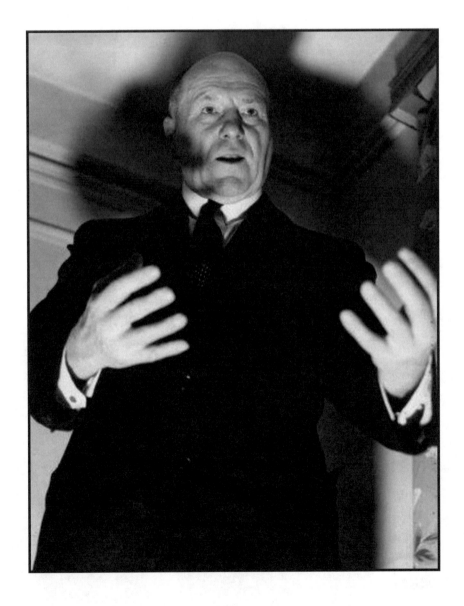

GOTCH
COMISKEY BALL PARK
HACKENSCHMIDT

GOTCH   HACKENSCHMIDT

WRESTLING CONTEST
AUSPICES EMPIRE ATHLETIC CLUB

PUBLISHED BOOKS

(JMILO EDICIONES AND AMAZON)

THE BOOK OF PROGRESSIONS

The Book of Progressions illustrates, with simple and concrete examples, how to design effective progressions, regressions, and variations for the most popular physical training exercises.

BIG3

The BIG3 Manual is specifically dedicated to the Deadlift, Squat, and Bench Press. It analytically explains the anatomical and functional processes underlying these three exercises and how to apply, transfer, and extrapolate this knowledge to other contexts.

GLUTES

The Book of Glutes provides an in-depth look at the connection between strength training and anatomical study. With a special focus on the gluteal muscles and their relationship to the rest of the body, this book is accessible and valuable for readers of all levels.

STRENGTH - ANATOMY - TRAINING 1

In the **first volume** of this comprehensive manual, the author explores in detail the connection between strength training and anatomical study. Using clear and understandable language, Jerónimo Milo manages to synthesize complex ideas. Readers will be able to apply this information in the context of physical activity, gaining a wealth of knowledge they can put to use right away.

STRENGTH - ANATOMY - TRAINING 2

Second Volume dedicated to the study of the Lower Limbs. The author provides an in-depth look at the connection between strength training and anatomical study. Thanks to the book's clear and understandable language, readers will be able to apply its information in the context of physical activity, gaining a wealth of knowledge they can put to use right away.

STRENGTH - ANATOMY - TRAINING 3

Volume 3 dedicated to the study of the Upper Limbs. In this comprehensive manual, the author provides an in-depth look at the connection between strength training and anatomical study. Using clear and understandable language, Jerónimo Milo manages to synthesize complex ideas. Readers will be able to apply this information in the context of physical activity, gaining a wealth of knowledge they can put to use right away.

KETTLEBELLS: FINAL EDITION

This **ultimate kettlebell manual** is one of the most complete collections on kettlebell training. Organized in a clear, intuitive way, it provides a quick and efficient approach to using kettlebells. Kettlebells: Final Edition serves as both an essential starting point and likely the only reference you'll need for kettlebell training.

FURIOUS AND UNCONVENTIONAL

In **The Kettlebell Manual: Furious and Unconventional** you'll gain access to unique, unconventional techniques that you can apply effectively to your training right away. The four ancient techniques introduced in this book, possibly the oldest known in kettlebell training, can readily become part of your workouts.

CLAVAPEDIA

Clavapedia is the first encyclopedia in Spanish on clubbell training. This work brings together the most extensive knowledge on the subject, covering both its ancient traditional forms and the Western style, both old and contemporary. It also explores possible variations and developments to achieve functional goals in modern training.

IVAN LEBEDEV

The book Kettlebell Exercises was originally published in 1928 in Moscow, in what was then the Soviet Union.

SECRET KETTLEBELL FILES

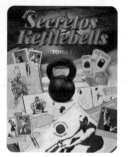

Kettlebell Secret Files is, without a doubt, the most comprehensive and detailed text on the origin, development, and evolution of kettlebell training.

ARTHUR SAXON

This time around, Jerónimo Milo not only provides an accurate translation of the original text, offering valuable lessons on weightlifting in its original form, but also takes us on a journey into the past, exploring details and anecdotes about the professional career and personal life of Arthur Saxon and his contemporaries.

THE WAY TO LIVE OF GEORGE HACKENSCHMIDT

Jerónimo Milo presents this work, **translated into Spanish for the first time**, enriched with his commentary and a compilation of extensive additional information from exhaustive research.

STATIC POSTURE MANUAL

In this static posture manual, you will find a simple and accessible approach to unlocking the secrets of static postures and standing meditation.

FREE DISTRIBUTION MANUALS

TRAINING GUIDE
KETTLEBELL FOR BEGINNERS

The **Training Guide: Kettlebell for Beginners** is a digital manual [PDF] written by Jerónimo Milo, created to freely provide essential information for starting kettlebell training effectively and safely.

TRAINING GUIDE
CLUBBELLS FOR BEGINNERS

The **Training Guide: Clubbells for Beginners** is a digital manual [PDF] written by Jerónimo Milo, aimed at freely disseminating the necessary information to start training with clubs effectively and safely.

FREE TURKISH GET-UP WITH KETTLEBELL MANUAL

Using the knowledge and tools presented in this **free** manual, start practicing the TGU right away. Learn to balance your levels of strength, mobility, and stability with this unparalleled exercise.

Made in the USA
Columbia, SC
23 January 2025

52108805R00113